RAISING KINGS

JACKIE GOUCHÉ

KP PUBLISHING COMPANY

ISBN: 979-8-9857184-9-2 (Paperback)
ISBN: 979-8-9857184-4-7 (eBook)
Library of Congress Control Number: 2022922126

Editor: Melanie James
Cover Design: Juan Roberts
Interior Design: Jennifer Houle
Literary Director: Sandra Slayton James

Published by:

KP Publishing Company
Publisher of Fiction, Nonfiction & Children's Books
Valencia, CA 91355
www.kp-pub.com

Printed in the United States of America

This book is dedicated to LaRenee Ervin, my "hang out and play with the boys" friend. For teaching me the difference between a lay-up and a jumper, and for showing me how to do both! For helping me to nurture my inner tom-boy, thereby causing me to be better equipped to be a single mother to three boys. For making me laugh heartier than anyone else I've ever known, and for telling me the truth even when I didn't want to hear it. Thank you for turning around and taking a picture of me and the boys that day we took them to the beach. And thank you for blurring the lines between sister/ friend/auntie and becoming such a part of my life that I wouldn't be who I am if we hadn't met.

Rest In Heaven

PRAISE FOR RAISING KINGS

It's been more than twenty years since I met Jackie Gouche. I remember sitting in church on Sunday mornings, listening to her beautiful voice and enjoying the service. Not long after, Jackie and I became friends, and I adopted her three boys into my heart and life like my own. I have had a front-row seat to the struggles and beauty of the Gouche-Farris family. It gives me no greater joy than to stand on the sidelines and watch as she shares her incredible story with the world. What Jackie and her sons have been able to overcome will serve as a source of strength, encouragement and inspiration to all who read it.

God bless you as you read ***RAISING KINGS!***

Tasha Smith
Actor, Director and Producer

CONTENTS

CPREFACE

God blessed me to give birth to some of the most amazing men one could ever have the pleasure of meeting. I've been told on numerous occasions that I have a magic uterus, and I believe there may be some truth in that statement. I am constantly humbled and in awe of who my sons have become.

Both Ronald and I came from broken homes with toxic environments plagued by alcoholism, drug addiction and poverty. Our religious but unhealthy culture was the experience of our grandparents and parents, and it eventually became a regular part of our childhood. We lived in a community where gang violence came with the territory, and safety was never guaranteed. Under these circumstances, we were still able to raise kings.

"How did you do it?" That is the question I often hear regarding my sons. Although I cannot personally take credit for their innate intelligence and gifts, their father and I did have something to do with the kind of men they have become.

We were fortunate enough to become parents just before the tide of social media swept through society. Cell phones were a luxury reserved for wealthy business executives. Laptops were merely bulky concept models that hadn't yet broken into the mainstream workflow. iPads were imaginary gadgets born from an obscure episode of The Jetsons or Star Trek. None of these technological advances even existed to tug at us in every free moment; there was no Instagram, Facebook, Tik Tok or Twitter. Our subconscious minds were not programmed to look toward mobile devices for entertainment; we inherently looked to one another. We went swimming, played card games, Scrabble, basketball in the park, took trips to the beach, played in the sand, rode bikes, go-karts, vacationed in the snow, played racquetball, went bowling, went to the batting cages, wrestled on the living room floor and tickled one another until we were unable to breathe. Quality time for us came naturally.

Today, there is always an LCD screen demanding our attention. Quality time has to be carefully planned and executed. The principles that govern human behavior are true whether you were born in the twentieth or twenty-first century. Although things are much different today than they were when I was raising my sons, principles don't change. The practices that worked for me in the eighties and nineties still work today. Things like; being attentive, patient and loving but firm, fearless, putting your children's needs before your own, teaching your babies everything you know, and guiding them to someone who can teach them what you don't know.

All of my experiences have reinforced the notion that spiritual principles, or laws, operate constantly whether you believe in them or not. Two laws that I believe have the greatest impact are (1) The Law of

Cause and Effect and (2) The Law of Compensation. Both of these laws remind us that our current circumstances are a direct result of our past choices. These two laws permeate every aspect of life. Alignment with them becomes especially vital during the early stages of parenting. Conversely, misalignment or complete ignorance of these laws may lead to the child suffering detrimental consequences for which the parent is responsible.

The Law of Cause and Effect says that for every action there is a corresponding reaction. Each reaction has a ripple effect that reaches far beyond our sphere of knowledge and lasts throughout our lives and beyond. The Law of Compensation primarily means that you will reap what you have sown. The respect that my sons have for me today is a direct result of the love I gave and the discipline that I exercised with them when they were very young. I was not a perfect parent, but I did parent them. I decided what was best for them and made it clear that I was the decision-maker until they were of the age where they could make their own decisions. And with each decision I made, I had their best interest at heart.

The success that my sons are experiencing now began the day I chose to sit them down as toddlers and teach them their ABCs, and the day I decided to stand my little ones around the piano and teach them music theory. The day I chose to turn down a Stevie Wonder tour to stay home and take care of my babies began a course of events that eventually led to them having a stable environment. This vital parental input they needed during their formative years allowed them to become spiritually and emotionally healthy people.

I knew how important it was to teach my toddlers how to read. I vividly remember my mother teaching me how to read long before I began attending school and, as a result, I was always one of the smartest girls in my class. But I must be honest with you and admit that at the time that I decided to teach them music, I was completely unaware of the impact it would have on their lives. I was just doing what I wished my parents had done for me. I started taking piano lessons when I was seven, but because I didn't like my teacher, I told my mother that I no longer wanted to take lessons, and she yielded. At the age of fourteen, when I reached high school, I was angry with her for not insisting that I continue with my piano lessons at age seven. So, I decided early that when I had children of my own, I would teach them music whether they wanted to learn it or not. Believe me, there were many times they didn't want to learn music, but I was the decision-maker in my home, and I didn't hesitate to enforce them.

RON RON

When I met my husband in 1983, he already had a son from his first marriage—Ronald II, or "Ron Ron" as he was affectionately called. Considering the majority of single parents are women, I thought it was admirable that Ronald was a single father, raising his son on his own. Ron Ron was nine years old when Ronald and I began dating. He was the most adorable little guy, and he welcomed me into his life as if it was meant to be. I was working as a waitress at the time. Ronald would bring Ron Ron to the restaurant to eat and to spend time with me. Ronald didn't tell me until after all our sons were born, but he prayed and asked God to give him only male children. God answered his prayers!

When people are expecting, they usually use the phrase "we're having a baby." Although that statement is fitting, it is thoroughly incomplete. You are not just having a baby . . . you are having a person! You are adding one more human being to the world, and you are responsible for what that person will either contribute to or take away from society. You are giving birth to either an asset or a liability. You hold within your womb a world of potential. The power to guide and shape that potential is in your hands.

It might have been nice if my husband and I had taken the time to carefully plan our family—deciding beforehand how many children we were going to have and when we would have them; but we didn't. At the tender age of 21, I gave birth to my first son, Davion. Daniel came only eleven months later, and thirteen months after Daniel, Sir Darryl was born. It's a good thing God knew what He was doing because Ronald and I certainly did not. Our children were simply the result of God's grace and good sex. We had our share of trials, but they did not stop us from making our sons a priority and eventually becoming the best parents we could be.

I've often asked myself if I had it to do all over again, would I do things differently? Would I wait until we were financially stable before having children? Would I carefully plan each pregnancy and space them out every three years? Or wait until we owned our own home before becoming parents? All of those choices seem to make perfect sense. But the honest answer is; I wouldn't change a thing. Our haphazard way of becoming a family led to three of the greatest blessings of my life. Becoming a mother to those boys became my reason for doing everything else I did. They were the motivation behind every goal that I was able to accomplish. That doesn't mean, however, that I would recommend that young couples today should do it the way we did. Absolutely not!

We live in a different time, with different values and a different economy. There was a time when one could graduate from college, get a good job, get married, buy a home, have 2.5 children, get a puppy, and live happily ever after. Those days are long gone. In today's society, with the cost of education, the scarcity of good jobs, the sweeping tide of social media, and skyrocketing housing prices, the old model is obsolete.

Parenthood is not for the faint of heart! It is not something to be entered into lightly. Being a parent is one of the most selfless things you can do. So, before conception, you need to ask yourself, "How selfish am I?" Once you become a parent, life as you know it is over. Before choosing to have children, you must consider whether or not you are willing to invest the massive amount of time that is necessary for being a good parent. Are you willing to place that tiny human being before yourself? Are you ready to give up a good night's sleep? Hanging out with your friends? Happy hour? Are you willing to make self-sacrifice a way of life? Even if you answered "no" to any or all of these questions, let me encourage you. Many of the qualities that you don't seem to possess, suddenly come naturally once you hold that little person in your arms. If you happen to be unexpectedly expecting, be of good cheer!

Because you are reading this book, more than likely, you know the outcome of our story—that Ron Ron, Davion, Daniel, and Sir Darryl Farris turned out to be some pretty incredible men. But what you may not be aware of is just how much we had to overcome on our journey of parenthood, which began while we were still in the midst of some extremely challenging circumstances. There was a myriad of elements that were at play in our lives during that time: broken families of origin, religion, drug addiction, and incarceration, to name a few. If I didn't tell the story, one would never know the hurdles we've conquered. Looking at our family from the outside, you might be astonished to know what it took to realize the life that we now enjoy.

In the pages to follow, I will share with you how the hand of God guided us while we were overcoming our challenges. His miraculous power not only kept us from destroying ourselves, and our children, but also blessed our family to successfully live out the destiny designed for us long before we were aware of it. I will also share with you the joys and challenges of learning how to navigate the awesome privilege of parenthood, and the wisdom we've gained in the process of *Raising Kings*.

INTRODUCTION

Music painted the walls of my childhood home. For most families, a record player or radio was the musical centerpiece. For my family, it was the piano. From my great grandmother to my children, the gift of music courses through our DNA. My mother's beautiful soprano voice echoed throughout our home as far back as I can remember. As I listened and watched her accompany herself on the piano, I did not yet grasp the magnitude of her incredible talent. She began singing and playing in church at the age of thirteen, and eventually traveled the world as a background vocalist. My mother, Betty Gouché, had a voice comparable to Aretha Franklin and was equally as skilled on the piano. She was briefly signed to Capitol Records, but her career as a solo artist never left the runway. She decided instead to stay home and focus on my brothers and me. She and my father had gotten a divorce when I was nine years old. It left me with a void that I would spend years trying to fill.

I started taking piano lessons at the age of seven, and my mother bought my brother, Andrew his first bass guitar when he was fourteen.

When it was time for me to attend high school, Andrew insisted that I enroll at Crenshaw High because of the music teacher, Mr. Bernie Dunlap. Mr. Dunlap was a brilliant classical pianist with an exceptional standard of musical excellence. He immediately took me under his wings and began giving me piano lessons, free of charge.

For the next three years, my relationship with Mr. Dunlap blossomed into a unique, father-and-daughter type of love affair. He taught and mentored me in all things music. He also presented me with every opportunity possible to perform and compete. The greatest of those experiences was when I auditioned for a performing arts group called the *Young Americans.*

I was accepted into the group and a few months after performing in our *New Kid Show,* I was asked to go on tour. In the second semester of my junior year in high school, I had the pleasure of traveling the country and performing Rogers and Hammerstein music with a group of young people from across the country. Milton Anderson, the founder of the group, would introduce me at the beginning of each show, "Here's sixteen-year-old Jackie Gouché . . . Jackie."

"Raindrops on roses and whiskers on kittens, bright copper kettles, and warm woolen mittens. Brown paper packages tied up with string, these are a few of my favorite things." This amazing, unforgettable experience would set the stage for the rest of my musical life.

The tour lasted five months. I had to attend summer school to make up the classes I missed. As I approached graduation, my plan was to attend college, get a music degree, then a teaching credential, and pattern my life after Mr. Dunlap. However, after the first semester at Long Beach State, I dropped out of school and headed in a different direction. There was an opening for a first soprano in the Praise the

Lord (PTL) Club with Jim and Tammy Faye Bakker. I sent an audition (cassette) tape singing *God is Truly Amazing*, by Denise Williams, and, within a week I was hired. At the age of eighteen, I moved to North Carolina, where I had the privilege of performing daily on national television. Monday through Friday, my mother and grandmother were filled with pride and excitement each morning as they turned to channel nine to watch me sing.

The thrill of being on television every day lasted for only a few months. I began to miss my family and my home in Los Angeles. It was during this time that I also felt my first inkling of the desire to become a mother. The void left over from my parents' divorce was still alive and well in me, and I imagined starting over with my own family.

When I pictured myself with children, I saw one girl, a mini-Jackie. I wanted to have a baby girl so that I could correct the mistakes I felt my mother had made with me. I understand that my mother did the best she could with the tools she had been given by her parents, but I learned some valuable lessons as a result of the things that happened to me as a child. Those experiences inadvertently prepared me to be the attentive, careful, focused mother that I would eventually become.

I envisioned myself showering my baby girl with all the love my mother gave me, and then some! My daughter would become my life. I wouldn't press her hair. I would patiently care for her natural curls until they grew down to her waist. I would find out early what her interests were, and support her as she pursued them, with music as a non-negotiable requirement. I would teach her to play the piano, and make sure she never gave up. I would teach her to sing, and we would sing together often. There was never a doubt in my mind that she would be vocally gifted, like her mother—and her mother—and her mother!

I wouldn't allow her to spend the night at the babysitter's house. I wouldn't go on any tours. I would be a stay-at-home mom until she left for college. I would hire tutors if necessary and make sure she attended the best schools. I would get to know her academic counselors so she would be prepared to succeed in her education. I would know what was going on in her life at all times and become acquainted with her friends, both male and female. I would make my house the place where they all wanted to hang out so I could keep an eye on her.

Long before I met my husband, I spent lots of time painting a vivid picture in my mind of what kind of mother I planned to be. Even though the picture never included sons, that is what became my reality—and what a beautiful reality it has been.

This is not a *how-to* book on parenting. It is simply the story of my experience in *Raising Kings*. How God, the Creator of the universe, empowered and enabled my husband and me to overcome seemingly insurmountable challenges including addiction, incarceration, and seven years as a single mom. It is the experience of a young, Black girl with dark skin and kinky hair, who grew up in an era where images of beauty did not include either of those qualities. As a result, this young Black girl suffered from low self-esteem and lacked confidence, except in one area. She had inherited the gift of music from her mother. That gift became her strength—it became her life. And she passed that gift on to her sons.

> *This one's for love, for mothers that's grievin', it's for that dreamer in that class that's underachievin'. It's for believers whose faith is all that's keepin' 'em breathin'. It's the Garden of Eden, it's for all of my heathens. This one's for Inglewood, both in Chicago and Cali. This*

one's for Manchester and Crenshaw, for Rally's. Happy moments happen to be sprinkled throughout half of these tragedies. Actually, I just start embracing change. It's safe to say that growth is an uncomfortable process and pain is a necessary investment for progress. I stress that if ever you get ill, or hurt against your will, it's just a quiz from God, this is our test, ah yes. This time it's gonna be different. I'll bless the world with honest quotes in every sentence and get better every moment just like Beverly mentioned. Hard times but never resentment, I stay forever relentless.

LET'S GO!

D Smoke

(Daniel Anthony Farris)

CHAPTER ONE
BABY BOYS

Ronald and I met three years after I graduated from high school, in the fall of 1983. I had just returned to Los Angeles from Charlotte, North Carolina, where I lived and worked as a PTL Singer for a year. Ron became a member of the church I attended as a teenager and developed a relationship with my mother and her sisters, Pat and Malinda, while I was away. My aunt Pat was concerned that I was a backslider because I didn't attend church often. So she asked Ronald if he would give me a call and help set me back on the right spiritual path. The first time Ronald called me, we spoke for several hours. By the end of the conversation, we both recognized that there was something special happening. We spoke again the next night and the next. This continued every night for two weeks until we finally decided to meet in person. Swept up in a whirlwind of a love affair, we were engaged within three months and I became pregnant in March of 1984. We were married the following month on April 27th.

Ronald and I were both passionate about our relationship with God and from my naïve perspective that was enough for us to have a successful, happy marriage. The first few months, however, were not at all what I anticipated. Like many other families, Ron had come from a home plagued by dysfunction. His mother fell prey to the heroin epidemic of the sixties, and was in and out of prison for most of his childhood, leaving him and his four siblings to be raised by their grandmother, Essie Burkley. When we first met, Ron had only been sober for eight months from an addiction to crack cocaine, and before our wedding day, he had begun using again. The idea of getting high was not foreign to me because as a teenager, smoking marijuana had been a daily habit. The frustration of dealing with a brand new husband who struggled with addiction made it easy for me to rekindle my relationship with weed.

We were forced to move out of our first apartment on 10th Avenue and Sixty-third Street because it was located right in the heart of a gang and crack-infested neighborhood. My mother, who had been a property manager for several years, got me a job managing a small apartment complex. What we didn't realize at the time was that we were going from the frying pan to the fire. The building was located on Gelber Place and Pinafore Street, in an area known as "the jungle." In 1984, the jungle was just that—a dense, tangled thicket full of wild-life. Drug deals, hustlers, and gang violence were common in that area and I was naïve to think that we could survive in such an environment.

During one of his brief periods of sobriety, Ronald appeared on a game show called Scrabble, hosted by Chuck Woolery. He came close to winning twenty-one thousand dollars, but only won six thousand. This was a blessing in disguise because had he won the larger amount, he may have smoked himself to death. When he received his winnings, he gave me two thousand dollars. He gave another two thousand to Grandma Essie and spent the last two thousand dollars on powdered cocaine.

I knew as soon as he received the money that he was going to get high. I was afraid he would disappear and didn't want the stress of worrying that something might happen to him, so I asked him to stay home. For five days straight, he cooked and smoked, without even taking a break to eat or sleep. After watching my husband spellbound by this drug, out of curiosity, I made the ill-fated decision to ask if I could "try" it. I put down my joint and picked up my husband's pipe, utterly unaware of the cesspool I was diving into. Ronald attempted to prevent me from taking my first hit, but the more he said "no" the angrier I became. How dare he try to tell me what I couldn't do, especially since he had been doing it non-stop for an entire week. What I should have been concerned about was becoming just like him. I don't know why that thought never crossed my mind but, after taking that first hit, all I could think about was taking another. I was immediately hooked. Fortunately, I had an appointment that day to get my hair braided in preparation for the birth of my first baby.

I spent five hours at the hair salon. It was difficult for me to focus because I kept wondering if Ron was going to run out of drugs before I got back home. As soon as the last braid was finished, I hurried home to satisfy the craving that had been stirring inside. By the time I got back, there was only enough cocaine to last for the rest of the day. That night we would do our best to settle back down and make a pathetic attempt at normalcy.

DAVION

Three weeks before my due date, on November 24th, 1984, around 11:30 p.m., I felt a tightening sensation that began in my abdomen and crept around to my lower back. It lasted only a minute or two, and at first, I didn't think much of it, until fifteen minutes later when it happened again. I looked at the clock and waited for it to subside. Still not sure what was going on, I waited. Exactly fifteen minutes later, it happened again and continued like clockwork for several hours. I knew I was in labor, but it wasn't really painful—at least not yet. It was just enough to keep me from getting a good night's sleep. I tried to stay in bed as long as I could, but by seven o'clock the next morning, the contractions were beginning to get closer and more intense.

At eleven o'clock in the morning, I was hit with my first real labor pain. It was severe enough to make me cry—more severe than any menstrual cramp I'd ever experienced, and I couldn't imagine it getting any worse. We called the hospital and they instructed us to wait until the contractions were five minutes apart before coming in. By that time, I thought I was dying and vowed that this baby would be an only child. We arrived at the hospital at 4 p.m., and they immediately whisked me off to the labor room where the nurse began putting an IV in my arm and strapping sensors to my stomach.

My mother never talked about what it was like to have a baby, so I had no frame of reference as I went through the labor process. Every conversation with the doctor and every article, or book I read up to this day was only theory. Whenever I'd heard the word contraction there was no real understanding. Nothing I ever imagined could have prepared me for what I was experiencing. It was painful, yet exciting, frightening, yet amazing! The feeling of being kicked from the inside is magical, and it is only outmatched by the exhilaration of meeting that little person for the first time. The only way for someone to know what it's like to give birth is to do it.

I don't remember the exact reason, but the doctor told me he wanted to avoid giving me an epidural, so I felt the full force of each contraction. Nurse Aimee was very attentive and sweet and made me feel as if she genuinely cared. I vividly remember her name because I yelled it out several times. I begged her to give me something for the pain with each contraction, which was more intense than the last.

Nurse Aimee got the okay from the doctor to give me something to help ease the pain. She injected a few milligrams of Demerol into my IV, which enabled me to get some rest. The relief only lasted for about an hour and I was too far dilated for them to give me anything else, so I had to tough it out until I reached at least nine centimeters.

"Can I push now?" I must have asked that question at least a dozen times before I heard the words "okay Mrs. Farris, it's time!" No one had ever told me that the muscles you use to push the baby out are the same ones involved in having a bowel movement. So, when I started pushing, I felt like I was doing something wrong.

"I'm so sorry!" I was woefully embarrassed and cried because of the mess I made.

"Don't worry Mrs. Farris, that's normal. It happens all the time," Aimee said as she simply cleaned up after me in one smooth swipe, without even wrinkling her brow. She tried to assure me that I had nothing to be embarrassed about, but it didn't matter what she said, I felt nothing but shame.

It took a while for me to push the baby out. It didn't help that he was three weeks premature. After pushing on and off for a good thirty minutes, at around 9 p.m., with Ronald standing right by my side, our precious gift finally arrived. A beautiful little chocolate drop with a head full of curly black hair and plump, purple lips, Davion Trenier Farris entered the world weighing in at only five pounds. He wasn't the girl I'd hoped for but the love I felt for that tiny person was more intense than anything I had ever known. There are no words to describe the amazing feeling that comes with bringing a new life into the world.

Up to this point in my life, nothing had been certain. My parents were divorced, so my experience of a family was unstable. I had dropped out of college, so I felt like a failure in my attempt at higher education. My job as a PTL singer ended as a result of racism, so my view of religion was tainted. I not only married an addict, but his addiction became my addiction, so my entire life seemed to lack stability. There were two things I was sure of; the unconditional love God had for me, and the deep, penetrating love I had for my son.

Davion came into the world with a calm personality. He was usually a pretty chill baby, crying only when his diaper needed changing or when he was hungry. Otherwise, he was content with his pacifier and the sound of the television or soft music, but that was not always the case. One night, when he was three weeks old, I couldn't get him to stop crying. His diaper was clean, and he had been fed and burped, but he continued crying—for hours. At 3 a.m., I found myself walking him back and forth in the living room, rocking him vehemently. By this time, we were both crying. Even though I was exhausted, I was crying because my baby clearly needed something, but I couldn't figure out what it was. I just walked, and rocked, and cried, and prayed . . . and walked some more, until his little voice weakened, and he finally found his way back to sleep.

Ronald and I tried our best to maintain a sense of normalcy, but the nature of addiction is such that no matter how good your intentions are, you usually find yourself doing the very thing that you hate. We had brief periods of abstinence, always interrupted by binges that lasted until we ran out of money. Constantly toggling between addiction and sobriety, we pulled ourselves together long enough to attend a few church services, and pretend that we were the good Christians everyone believed us to be. We weren't able to keep up the pretense for very long. My mother had been accustomed to hearing from me nearly every day, and she became suspicious when several days would go by without a phone call. She sensed that something was wrong and decided to come by the apartment to check on us. Nothing could have prepared her for what she found. My five-foot, seven-inch frame was accustomed to holding a hundred and fifty pounds, but I had dwindled to a mere one twenty-five. It didn't take much for her to figure out that something was seriously wrong.

"Pack your things, you're coming with me." My mom didn't ask if I wanted to go, and she wasn't going to take no for an answer.

"What about Ronald?" I asked.

"What about him? I don't know where he's going to go, but he has to leave this apartment right now!" My mom was furious. She knew Ronald from church and, like me, thought he would have made a great husband. Neither of us was prepared for the baggage that came along with this union. We had only known alcohol and marijuana in our past and were unfamiliar with the devastating impact of cocaine addiction. I packed up all of my clothes, Davion's playpen, and toys and went home with my mother. It was a relief to have been rescued from that chaotic cycle. I felt bad for leaving Ronald with nowhere to go, but I

7

couldn't help him—I could barely help myself. I knew that leaving him and moving in with my mom was the best thing I could do, especially since I had become pregnant with our second child between binges.

My mom only had a one-bedroom apartment, so Davion and I slept in the living room. I fought daily against feelings of worthlessness. The only thing that kept me from losing my sanity was my beautiful baby boy. Ronald pulled himself together and moved back in with Grandma Essie. He found his way back to sobriety for a few months, and since we were expecting our second child, we decided to give our marriage another try. We asked my dad if we could move in with him until we were able to afford our own place.

Ike Gouché owned a tiny house with two bedrooms and one bathroom located on Seventh Avenue and Sixtieth Street. My dad's experience in construction made him believe himself to be the consummate do-it-yourself-er, often beginning remodeling projects and never finishing them. He was quick to tear down walls, replace pipes or pull up old tile. There were times when an entire year went by before the new tile was installed. The drywall in the kitchen remained unfinished, with only white primer over the nails. My dad replaced the old bathtub with a new one, but never replaced the surrounding tile, and you could see right through to the plumbing. Despite the rough edges, we were grateful to have a place to land.

DANIEL

In the spring of 1985, I received a call from Sandra Crouch, inviting me to sing on the soundtrack for the movie *The Color Purple*. We provided the voices for the scene where Shug was running to try and keep Celie from cutting Mister's throat. Also, for the choir scene in the song *God*

Is Trying to Tell You Something. A few months later, in September (when I was seven months pregnant), I received another call. The voice they had previously used for the solo of the young girl in the choir stand didn't match the face of the actor, so they needed a younger sound. They asked me to replace her voice and I was thrilled!

"Yeeeeeees, yeeeeeeees, yes Lord . . . my soul, my soul says ye-e-es . . . if I were you I would say yes!" The raw footage of that scene in the movie played on a large screen while we recorded the audio. I viewed it several times because I had to match the actor's movements perfectly. The experience was surreal, almost making me forget my addiction. But that feeling only lasted until I received the payment for the session. It was more money than I had ever made at one time and the only thing I could think of was how much cocaine I could buy with sixteen hundred dollars. Soon Ronald and I were once again living that same chaotic cycle. I blamed him for my drug habit and thought that I would be able to control myself if he weren't there. I asked him to leave, but that did not solve my problem. I continued to smoke while Ronald checked himself into the rehab program at the Veterans Hospital in Westwood.

The binge that began with the money from *The Color Purple* session didn't last nearly as long as I expected. I had run out of money and drugs within a few days and was left swimming in a sea of guilt and self-hatred for having smoked so much during my pregnancy. It was a vicious cycle. Whenever I received money, the cravings were so strong that the only thing that made them stop was to get high. Then came the extreme guilt I felt for lacking the ability to control myself. The quickest way to get rid of the guilt was to get high again. As long as I was high, I felt nothing but euphoria. Coming down was like being in a plane crash.

When I received my welfare check on October 15th, 1985, I bought enough food, diapers, and milk to last for the rest of the month and was left with forty dollars. Even that small amount of money stirred up that feeling in my gut that could only be soothed by a hit. So, at ten o'clock in the morning on October 17th, I packed up my baby in the stroller and walked all the way from Sixtieth Street and Seventh Avenue to the dope house on Slauson and Normandie, exchanged my last forty dollars for one tiny piece of rock cocaine, then turned around and headed back home.

I'd convinced myself that this was going to be the absolute last time I would get high, and I planned on enjoying it. I changed and fed Davion, then rocked him until he went to sleep. It was my way of trying to be a good mother, despite my deplorable circumstances. As soon as he was asleep, I went into the bathroom, closed the door, and began smoking. I had somehow prepared my mind for the end. So, when I took my last hit and there was nothing left to smoke, I didn't waste time scraping the pipe and crawling around on the floor looking for crumbs. I went into the kitchen, got a can of white paint, a roller, and a pan. I needed to be productive, to do something that gave me a sense of worth. The smell of the paint was almost as intoxicating as the pipe, which was strangely comforting. The squishing sound it made as I rolled it over the drywall also had a soothing, hypnotic effect. I finished the first wall, and, for a brief moment, I almost felt good about myself. Just before starting on the second wall, I felt a tightening sensation that began in my abdomen and crept around to my lower back.

"Oh God, not now!" I knew immediately that I was going into labor, but it was way too soon. The baby wasn't due for another five weeks—not to mention the fact that I had just finished smoking. I lied down on the couch and prayed that there would be no more contractions but about ten minutes later, it happened again. I kept praying, but the contractions kept coming, and they were closer and more intense than the first time around. I called my father and told him I was going into labor. He left work immediatcly and headed home. I also put in a call to the Veteran's Hospital and left a message for Ronald to meet me at Kaiser.

By the time my father got home, the contractions were already five minutes apart. Being in labor made it easy to hide the fact that I was terrified. I didn't want my dad to know that I had gotten high just a couple of hours ago, so I pretended that my tears were caused by the contractions. The reality was that I was afraid that they were going to find drugs in my baby's system and immediately take him away from me. I pictured myself being handcuffed in a hospital gown and carted off to jail as soon as he was born. The contractions began to intensify much faster than they had the first time around. We arrived at the hospital around four in the afternoon, and Ronald showed up a few minutes later. The contractions were now coming every three minutes, so they rushed me off to labor and delivery and immediately hooked me up to the fetal monitor. My father took care of Davion while Ronald stayed by my side. Neither of them was aware of how I'd spent my morning, and I didn't want to let them in on my dirty little secret.

I cried nearly the entire time I was in labor, and between each contraction, and every tear, I prayed. I knew just enough about God to know that He still loved me, and that He would forgive me if I asked him to. I must have asked Him a thousand times. I prayed that they wouldn't find drugs in my baby and take him away from me. I asked God to protect his mind and prayed that he would come out normal and healthy, with all ten fingers and toes.

11

"God, I know that I have no right to ask you for anything right now, but please, *please* don't let them take my baby? Please let him be okay? I'm so sorry for . . ." There was so much that I was sorry for, I didn't know where to begin. I was sorry for allowing my curiosity to overwhelm me, and for asking Ronald to let me *try* it. I was sorry that I had been unable to control myself, and that I was just as addicted as he was. I was sorry for the damage that I may have potentially caused my unborn child. I was just so sorry! Ronald was at my bedside rubbing my back and my feet, massaging my temples, and feeding me ice chips. He was doing everything in his power to help me through this difficult process.

The contractions were now coming every minute, and the pain was so intense that I was no longer worried about that morning. I had prayed and cried, and prayed some more, and a strange peace came over me that I could not explain. I had let go of my guilt and was ready to give birth to a normal, healthy baby. I don't remember the nurse's name because this time, instead of calling her, I whispered a silent prayer of thanksgiving as each labor pain subsided. My gratitude began to overwhelm my guilt. The support of my father and my husband, and the knowledge that my mother would be there for me is what gave me strength. Most of all, I knew that God would never give up on me.

"Lord, I know that you've heard every one of my prayers, and I thank you for your love and mercy. Thank you for blessing this child in spite of me!"

At around eight o'clock that night, four hours after arriving at the hospital, little Daniel Anthony Farris arrived. The labor was much shorter, and I didn't have to push nearly as long and hard as with Davion. This time I knew exactly what to expect, having just done it eleven months prior. The closer I got to ten centimeters, the more I asked myself "what were you thinking Jackie?" You knew how painful this was!"

As soon as Daniel came out, I forgot all about the pain. Once they made sure he was breathing clearly, the doctor immediately placed him on my chest. And just like the first time around, the love I felt was overwhelming. Tears began to flow as I held my second baby boy. Daniel weighed only four pounds, but he was otherwise normal, healthy, and beautiful!

The doctor had to press down on my stomach to get the placenta out and it was more painful than the actual birth. As soon as it was over, they took Daniel for the routine tests given to each newborn and wheeled me to my room where I went straight to sleep. A few hours later, I woke up almost in a panic. The sense of peace I felt before Daniel's birth had disappeared. I was alone in my room with no one in sight. I felt a strange void after being pregnant, then waking up with no baby in my stomach or my arms.

Ronald was not allowed to stay out overnight because of the rules of his rehab program, so he'd left while I was sleeping. I got out of bed, put on my robe and slippers, and went to find my baby. As I walked down the long hallway, I was relieved that there were no police waiting to arrest me. There was, in fact, only an eerie silence. I made my way around the corner to find the nurse sitting quietly at her station just outside the nursery.

"Hey Mrs. Farris, did you sleep well?" she said with a smile on her face.

"Yes, I did. How's my baby?" I said, still nervous about whether or not I had caused some type of damage.

"Your baby is fine. He's right there, sleeping peacefully," she said as she stood and pointed to the acrylic crib that held my tiny little guy.

"Did you check him . . . is he okay?" I wasn't quite sure how to phrase my question. I wanted to know if they found any drugs in his system.

"Yes, we checked him. He's a little small, but otherwise, he's absolutely perfect." I breathed a huge sigh of relief.

"Can I hold him?" I asked.

"Of course you can! He's *your* baby!" She headed to the crib located in the middle of the room between the other new arrivals. She picked little Daniel up and handed him to me. I was overcome with relief and joy. He looked like a little man, with chiseled features. His little nose was straight and defined, just like his father's.

"Thank you" I whispered as I took my son and held him close to my breast.

"Can I take him to the room with me?" I asked, still a little apprehensive about everything.

"Here," she said as she reached out her arms.

"Give him to me and I'll bring him to you in your room." It was against the rules for them to allow me to walk around carrying the baby. So, I headed back to my room and got in bed. The nurse was right behind me, rolling little Daniel in his crib. Once I was settled, she handed him to me, along with a bottle of formula to feed him. The sense of relief was even greater than the relief I felt after that final push. I was so grateful to be holding my son in my arms, with the assurance that he was perfectly whole and healthy. Once again, God had answered my prayers.

Daniel and I were released from the hospital the next day. My father came to pick us up, with little Davion strapped in his car seat in the back of his Chevy van. He had purchased a second car seat for little Daniel. I was grateful that my dad was there for me. I don't know what I would have done without him.

Except for a few episodes of colic, and a couple of ear infections, Davion was an easy little guy, like Sunday morning. Daniel, on the other hand, was more like Saturday night! He came into the world like a boss. He cried all the time . . . for no reason, so I thought. It didn't take me long to figure out that he was crying because he had not yet learned to talk and was frustrated with the fact that he was unable to communicate what he was feeling.

I bought Davion a playpen and was accustomed to him spending lots of time in it. All he needed was his little brown teddy bear, a few teething toys, some music, and he was fine. But Daniel didn't understand the concept of a playpen. It must have felt more like a prison to him, and he made it clear by standing on his tippy toes with his hands gripped firmly on the railing, tensing his entire body, looking directly at me, and screaming at the top of his lungs until I took him out. There were no tears. He wasn't crying, he was just screaming! He was only about eight months old and could barely talk or walk, but he knew what he wanted . . . and what he didn't want. Daniel was teaching me the important lesson that each child came with his own set of rules, and what worked for one was not guaranteed to work for the other. I began to understand that I had two unique humans—each with their own personality, their own style of *being* in the world.

After Ronald left the rehab program at the VA, he got a job cleaning a church in the city of Pomona. This was the best possible move he could have made, because not only had he found a job keeping the church clean, but the Pastor allowed him to live there as well. Of course, he was required to attend Sunday services, but he welcomed the idea. Each time Ronald got paid, he would borrow the Pastor's car and drive down to Los Angeles to see me, and the boys. He made sure we had everything we needed; diapers, milk, food, and even a little cash. Ronald wasn't getting high, so with every visit, he became more and more appealing to me. He had gained a little more weight and had a healthy glow about him. Having two brand new sons motivated him to do what was necessary to get himself together.

Papa, the pastor of the church, had become quite fond of Ronald. When he learned that Ron had a wife and three sons, he was willing to do everything within his power to help us. He spoke to one of the mothers of the church who agreed to rent us a room in her home. So, I hugged my dad and thanked him for all he'd done for me, then packed up my two baby boys, and we moved to Pomona to be with Ronald.

For a few months, it appeared as if our lives were back to normal. Ronald was working hard every day keeping the church clean and assisting the Pastor with any and everything he needed to have done, while I was at home taking care of the babies. We attended church every Sunday and I even sang from time to time. But I was only pretending to be fulfilled with the life we were living. So far removed from what I had imagined for myself, being a stay-at-home mom with two babies, married to a man who worked as a janitor. Our circumstances were somewhat humiliating. Not as bad as being strung out on drugs, but still so far below my potential. I constantly battled depression.

On the first and fifteenth of each month, we borrowed Papa's car and drove to Los Angeles to pick up my county check from my father's house. For a couple of months, we were able to keep our cravings at bay, but we both had yet to reach our rock-bottom and get to the point where we were able to completely put our relationship with cocaine behind us. On our fifth trip to Los Angeles, the tension in the car was palpable, dark, and heavy. Without saying a word, we agreed that this would be the day that we'd give in to our cravings. The beast within had been starved long enough and it was time to feed it. After cashing the check, Ron pulled into the parking lot on Century and La Brea to formulate a plan.

"Okay . . . we are only going to spend fifty dollars and then head back up the hill to Pomona," Ronald told that lie, and we both pretended to believe it. The reality was that neither of us cared enough about the consequences to admit the truth, that once we got started, we wouldn't stop until all the money was gone.

Our actions that night were the beginning of the destruction of everything Ronald had built for us in Pomona, including the Pastor's trust and our reputation at the church. We carefully crafted enough lies to carry us for two more weeks but by the time we went to pick up the next check we were so far gone that we had reached the point of no return. We failed to pay the rent for that month and were forced to find another place to live. Fortunately for us, there was no connection between the church in Pomona and our old church in Los Angeles. So, word of our addiction had not yet gotten back to our original pastor, who helped us find a place to live. There was another member who was willing to rent us a room in their new home. They thought it would be a good idea because they had gotten in over their heads and could use the extra help with the mortgage payment.

Bill and Laura welcomed us with open arms, completely unaware of the fact that they were inviting two drug addicts into their home, and all the drama that came along with us. They agreed to allow us to pay them biweekly, so we gave them the money for the first two weeks. That would be the only payment we made. When the time came for us to make another payment, we didn't have a dime. We had a huge fight over the last thirty dollars, and I packed up the two babies and left Ronald in the middle of the night after he'd drunk himself to sleep. I headed back to my father's house where I knew I would be accepted and loved.

BETTY GOUCHÉ

CHAPTER TWO

DARK DAYS

Shortly after moving back in with my father, we received a call from my aunt Malinda. She was struggling to raise her five children on her own and also needed a place to live. My father was a gracious, generous man and had always been willing to help my mother's younger siblings. So, he slept on the couch and allowed Malinda and I, and all seven of our children, to have the two bedrooms. I began attending church again with Malinda and, within a few days, the hope of a normal life was becoming more and more a reality. I prepared myself to raise my two sons on my own, but I soon realized that I had become pregnant again during our sober days in Pomona.

As much as I loved my two beautiful baby boys, I was neither ready nor willing to handle a third child. I immediately planned to have an abortion and go on with my life as a mother of two. I made the appointment without giving it a second thought, but my Aunt Malinda wasn't having it. She begged me not to go through with the abortion, promising to help me every step of the way. She made me agree that if

God answered her prayers and provided us with a decent place to live, then I would keep the baby. She had it all figured out.

"When we get our next checks, God is going to bless us to find a house for rent, and I promise to help you when the baby is born." My Aunt Malinda was full of faith and enthusiasm regarding her plan. Although I agreed with her verbally, inside I was convinced that no one in their right mind would rent a house to two single welfare mothers with seven children. I intended to go through the motions of searching for a place to rent. As soon as her plan failed, my plan was to keep my appointment at the abortion clinic and then find a way to get high.

A few days later, on the first of the month, we borrowed my mother's little orange 1979 Chevrolet Monza, packed up our seven children, and set out in search of a place to live. We had to wait until our checks came in the mail, so we didn't leave the house until late in the afternoon. We stopped at the AM PM Mini Market to pick up copies of the *L.A. Times* and *Recycler* newspapers and began our search in the classified section. We circled a few rental ads and drove by each of them, but with no success. Several hours passed and we still had not found a house, so we started looking at apartments. At around eight o'clock that night, Malinda made what I initially thought was an insane declaration.

"We prayed for a house! Why are we looking at apartments?" She went back over the ads in the *Recycler* and found one that we somehow overlooked. *"Three-bedroom, one-bath house, $675,"* we found the nearest payphone and called the number. Mr. Segura, the owner of the house, agreed to meet us immediately. As we waited for him to arrive, I felt hopeful that this could be the miracle Malinda had prayed for. Sure enough, without filling out an application, and only one month's rent, Mr. Segura gave us the keys to the house. We rushed back to my father's house to pick up some clothes and toiletries and, that night, we slept on the floor of our miracle.

After two years of living in chaos, living with Malinda was refreshing. Every morning, she would get up early and pray before sending her older boys off to school. Her prayers were fervent, passionate, sincere, and loud! Initially, I would stay in bed and listen, feeling like a spiritual failure because I was not the prayer warrior that Malinda was. Before long, her prayers inspired me to get out of bed, fall to my knees and begin to develop my own consistent line of communication with God. It was surprising when I realized just how much peace and strength I gained through prayer, despite my recent behavior. Other than being in a house and being sober, not much about my circumstances had changed. I was still a single, welfare mother. My life consisted of taking care of two babies, taking care of myself in preparation to have a third one, and going to church. From the outside looking in, I may have appeared somewhat pathetic, but deep down inside, I knew the value of those little lives I was responsible for, and I was determined to provide them with every opportunity to have a better life than the one I was living.

While Malinda and I were enjoying our new home, Ronald hit such a low point in his addiction that he made an unsuccessful suicide attempt. He was admitted into the mental health facility at the VA hospital and stayed there for 90 days. My last words to him before moving back in with my father were that our marriage was over. During his stay at the VA, he met a woman. They started dating almost immediately, and he moved in with her after being released from the 90-day program. I was angry with him because of the trauma we experienced, and although I didn't want to be his wife, I certainly didn't want to see him with another woman. It was unfair! I was the one carrying his third child and I felt like he owed it to me to make me, and his sons, his first priority.

He would visit us regularly, bringing money, milk, and diapers. He would also spend time playing with Davion and Daniel, before returning home to his other woman. I was an emotional basket case. Overwhelmed with anger, resentment, and jealousy, I could hardly interact with him during his visits. Malinda was a strong source of support for me. She encouraged me to simply pray and trust God to work it out. That was her answer for everything. It seemed trite and redundant at first, but after a few months of following her advice, I was once again at peace, even though Ronald was still living with his girlfriend.

In early November of 1986, my frustration level had reached a peak. With only eleven months between the births of my first two children, I felt like I had been pregnant for three whole years, and I was ready for it all to be over. Like Davion and Daniel, Sir Darryl was premature, and this delivery would be the most difficult of them all. The baby wasn't due until January third, but on the fourth of November, I felt a tightening sensation that began in my abdomen and crept around to my lower back. It was a familiar feeling, and I knew exactly what was happening only this time, I welcomed it. We called the hospital and they told me to come in right away. The doctor wanted to give me something to stop the contractions because it was way too early. Although every cell in my body was ready to bring this pregnancy to an end, I obeyed the doctor's orders and headed for the hospital. I called Ronald and he was there waiting for me when I arrived.

They wheeled me directly into the exam room where they gave me an ultrasound. I wasn't sure why, but I saw it as an opportunity to find out if I would finally have the daughter that I dreamed of. Little Sir must have had his third leg neatly tucked away, because they somehow missed it, and told me I was having a girl. Immediately after the ultrasound, they hooked me up to an IV and began administering a drug to stop the contractions. It only worked slightly, and not for very long. The contractions continued for the next eight hours. At this point, my frustration level had reached a peak and I begged the doctor to stop giving me that drug and allow nature to take its course. The thought of going back home with the baby still in my stomach was unbearable. After about four more hours of consistent, mild contractions, the doctor finally agreed to stop giving me the ineffective drug.

Shortly thereafter, the intensity of the contractions increased slowly. It would take another ten hours before I was ready to give birth to what I thought was my baby girl. Ronald had been by my side the entire time and was standing right next to me, holding my hand when Sir Darryl came on the scene. After twenty-two hours of labor, and one final push, it was all over. Exhausted and relieved from the experience of giving birth to my third baby in a row, I didn't bother to look up. I simply laid back and closed my eyes for a moment. When I opened them, I saw a troubled look on Ronald's face.

"It's not a boy, is it?" I said, fearing the answer to that question. "It's a boy" Ronald replied in a worried tone. It felt like I had been sucker-punched! Why would God do that to me? Why would they tell me he was a she? They whisked my tiny little boy away to make sure he was breathing sufficiently. Although he only weighed three pounds, his little lungs were strong. His cry echoed throughout the room—it was a beautiful sound.

When the tears finally subsided and they placed that tiny little boy in my arms, I instantly felt the same love for him that I had for his brothers. I immediately thought of the fact that I had almost ended his life before it began, and the tears of disappointment turned into tears of joy and gratitude. I wanted to name him Darryl, in keeping with the letter D, but Ronald's mother, grandma Mattie insisted that we call him *Sir Darryl*.

He weighed only three pounds, but Sir Darryl Andrew Farris was otherwise a perfectly healthy baby. Because he was so small, they had to keep him in the hospital, monitoring him until he weighed at least four pounds. Initially, I was relieved that I would get the chance to rest for a few days before bringing him home. But the first night at home without my baby felt wrong. I believed he was in good hands, but they weren't mine. I was confident that he was receiving the health care he needed, but I was certain that he was *not* getting the love and affection that a newborn so desperately needs. Nights without my newborn were difficult and sleep escaped me. I went to the hospital every day for two weeks until he had gained enough weight to go home with me.

Sir was so tiny. I would hold him with one hand, his little head resting in my palm, his back on my forearm and his little legs dangling at my elbow. When I was finally able to bring him home, I felt complete. I would lay my three beautiful baby boys down to sleep and just watch as their little tummies rose and fell. With each breath, sigh, smile, or whimper, I was more and more in awe of the great responsibility that lay before me. Part of me was concerned that I might not have what it takes to raise them properly. But my instincts said that Sir Darryl Andrew, Daniel Anthony, and Davion Trenier were now my reason for existing. Whatever I may have lacked, I somehow knew that God would be there to provide it.

As a newborn, Sir Darryl was the least demanding of all of my sons. Once he had eaten, all was right with the world. Naptime was interesting. I tried my best to get them all to go to sleep at the same time, but that didn't happen very often. It turned out, however, to be a good thing. I used it as an opportunity to spend precious time with each of my baby boys individually, while the other two slept. I would make up songs and sing to them, looking forward to the day that they would be able to sing along with me.

"Dan, Dan, the honey man! Dan, Dan, the funny man! Dan, Dan, the mini man, Dan, Dan the skinny man." Each of them had their own personal mommy time song and it was their laughter that kept me alive.

"Ride hobby horse, downtown, take care of little Sir, don't fall down. Buckety, buckety, buckety, buckety. . ." I sang this while bouncing him on my knee. I used the melody to *Edelweiss*, from *The Sound of Music* and re-wrote the lyrics, especially for Davion.

"Davion, Davion, every morning you greet me. Small and brown, sweet and round, I'm so happy you need me!" I found the greatest joy in the smiles on the faces of my three little guys. I also found the strength to fight the desire to get high. My love for my sons was incentive enough for me to stay sober. Unfortunately, Ronald had been arrested for possession and was in the county jail. His addiction had completely taken him over and I was now left with the responsibility of caring for my boys without their father, but I was not alone. My mother and my Aunt Malinda were there to help me whenever I needed them.

Dinnertime was simple. As soon as little Sir was able to sit up by himself, I would sit on the couch with all three of the boys on the floor in front of me and feed them out of one plate or bowl. They were six months, a year and a half, and two and a half years of age. For several months, my days consisted of; feeding, bathing, dressing, changing, potty training, tickling, kissing, and playing with my baby boys. I didn't have a nine-to-five job, so the thought of day-care never crossed my mind. During this season, my only job was motherhood, and whenever there was a need that my welfare check could not cover, my mother was there to make up the difference.

Now and then I looked in the mirror and wondered how the hell I ended up in this position. I was gifted, intelligent, and driven. But I had dropped out of college and started on an uncharted path of marriage, motherhood, and addiction. Over the next five years, I found myself a single, welfare mother with four sons. This is certainly not what I planned. I was supposed to be a college graduate and music teacher, well on my way to becoming a professor. I only felt frustration when I looked in the mirror, or when it was time to pay bills. When I looked at my boys, however, all I felt was joy. It didn't matter that my own life was not turning out the way I'd hoped it would. I was now responsible for shaping three little lives, and I was determined to give them everything I had.

After living with Malinda for several months, my life had stabilized to the point where I was convinced that addiction was a thing of the past, until the thirteenth of September 1987. Malinda came into my bedroom around four in the morning. With tears in her eyes, she handed me the phone. It was my brother, Anthony, calling me with the worst possible news.

"Daddy is dead" he said, his voice shaking.

"Somebody shot him . . . He's dead." There was nothing that could have prepared me for that moment. My mind was not willing to accept what I was hearing.

"NOOOOOOOOOOOO!!!" I dropped the phone and screamed. This pain was worse than anything I'd ever experienced in my life. It was as much physical as it was emotional, cutting to the core of my soul and radiating out to every part of my body. My scream woke up the boys, and they immediately began to cry. They didn't know how to handle seeing their mother like this. Malinda took them into the living room and comforted them, while I curled up in a ball and continued to cry until I had no more strength. My mother and my two older brothers arrived at our house within an hour. The only thing that made sense was for us to be together at this moment. We held one another and cried, still in disbelief of what just happened. We did our best to try and comfort each other, but there was really nothing to be said or done to make things better.

After a couple of hours, my mom and my brothers went home, and I drove over to the place where our father had taken his last breath. It was on Buckingham Road between Martin Luther King Boulevard and Santa Rosalia Drive in Los Angeles. He had been hanging out on the porch drinking with some of his friends, his car parked in the alley around the corner. They were still standing around, grappling with what had taken place the previous night. One of his friends described the events leading up to my father's murder. As I listened to him speak, I kept wishing that I could wake up from this nightmare.

"We were just sitting here on the porch kickin' it and talking about old times. It must have been just after midnight when he decided to leave. He walked right over there," he said, pointing to the alley.

"Not even a minute passed before I heard the shots. I ran over to see what was going on, and there he was, lying on the ground. I picked his head up and held him, trying to talk to him until the ambulance came, but he died in my arms . . . I'm so sorry baby girl. I wish there was something I could have done." Even though I didn't know him, I felt a strange connection to the last man to see my father alive. It was almost as if I could still feel my dad's heart beating as he spoke.

The following week was a blur. Going through the motions of living, I became accustomed to the constant, excruciating pain of losing my father. Someone had taken him away from me, and it could not be undone. A few days went by before we were allowed to go and see his body in the mortuary. Malinda took care of the boys while I went with my uncles Trenier and Calvin, and my grandma Woodland, to see him. The drive seemed like an eternity, and I don't remember any of the conversations that took place on the way. All I knew was that I was going to see the dead body of the man I had called *daddy* for my entire life, a notion that still felt unreal.

The pleasantries of the mortuary attendants were annoying. I realized that they were only trying to be helpful, but their efforts were futile.

"Would you like to go in alone, Ms. Gouché?" The attendant pointed the way into the room while my uncles and grandmother stood back and allowed me to go in first. I didn't really know what to expect. I had never actually seen a corpse before. The closer I got to the casket, the more I realized that I was not looking at my father. I reached out to touch him, but when I felt the cold, hard matter that was once my dad, that's when I realized *he* wasn't there. I immediately turned and left the room. There was no point in spending time with the shell that my father once lived in.

For the next few days until the funeral, I tried my best to keep myself together for my babies, but underneath every breath and every thought was the desire to rid myself of the pain, and I only knew one way to do that. To me, the funeral was only a formality. I had already said goodbye to my dad at the mortuary a few days earlier. Ronald was unable to attend my father's funeral because he was still in jail on the possession charge.

My brother, Anthony, gave the eulogy. He talked about the fact that our father was a wonderful provider. He always made sure we had everything we needed. We were actually able to laugh a bit when he talked about my dad's crude mannerisms and often profane way of speaking. But there was no doubt that he loved us, and he always made sure we knew it.

I received several sympathy cards, some containing a small cash gift. The total was $85. I couldn't wait to get home and ask Malinda to watch the boys so that I could get away for a while. I told her I just needed to take a walk and that I would be gone for no more than thirty minutes. As I left home and headed toward the dope house, the desire to numb my pain far outweighed thoughts of the possible consequences of my actions. The ache that permeated every part of my body and soul could only be soothed by one thing. I was willing to pay whatever the price, even though I knew the relief would only be temporary.

The dope spot was a familiar place; I had purchased and smoked there many times. With my father's obituary still in my hand, I sat down at the table and began smoking. Just as I had anticipated, the pain went away. For about ninety seconds, I felt nothing. My mind was blank, and my body was at ease. I closed my eyes and took a few deep breaths in an attempt to savor the moment, but it swiftly passed and the ache to which I had become so familiar began to return. It was time for another hit.

This cycle went on for about twenty-four hours. I had run out of cocaine and ways to get more so I decided it was time to go home. The three-block walk felt like three miles. Initially relieved to bring that binge to an end, I opened my front door, only to find my brother, Anthony, there waiting for me with a barrage of questions and accusations. He was livid! He couldn't understand how and why I would put the family through such trauma immediately after losing our dad.

"How could you do that to us?" He yelled. "You don't care about anybody but yourself!"

"Anthony, you don't understand!" I tried to explain my position, but none of it made any sense to him. He continued attacking me, both verbally and physically.

"WHY DON'T YOU JUST STOP! YOU CAN STOP IF YOU WANT TO! YOU JUST DON'T WANT TO!" Anthony screamed as he tightened his grip around my neck. Thankfully, Malinda was there to intervene. He was definitely not helping the situation, he only made me want to go back to the dope house and get numb again. Malinda was able to calm him down and get him to leave. After he left, she came into my room where I was curled up on my bed, sobbing. She placed her hand on my back and began speaking softly and lovingly to me.

"Jackie, I know you're sorry, so you don't have to say it. I've already forgiven you and God will too, all you have to do is ask Him." Malinda understood that I was fighting for my life and that it would be impossible for me to win that battle alone. She did her best to support me as I recovered from that last episode.

Within a week, the overwhelming guilt of my addiction began to subside. The pain of losing my dad was still fresh, but I no longer had a desire to ease it with cocaine. The temporary reprieve was not worth the aftermath. I shifted my focus to my old familiar friend, music. Sitting down at the piano, I began to write.

"I'll never know why, why you did what you did. You didn't have to die, but you did. You hung on the cross so that I wouldn't be lost. You took my place, now you're pleading my case. You didn't have to do it, Oh but I'm glad you did, you didn't have to do it, but I'm glad you did." It was as if the song was already written, and I was simply the instrument through which it was played.

Within a few weeks, I received a call from an old friend and producer, Scott Smith. He was looking for music for a new artist by the name of Crystal Lewis. They both loved the song, and we immediately went into the studio to record it.

The experience of having someone record one of my songs gave me a new sense of worth, reminding me of the gifts I possessed. It wasn't long before I felt normal again. The responsibility of caring for my children helped me to stay focused.

The fact that those three little people were completely dependent upon me is what gave me strength. I began attending church again with Malinda, with the belief that it would make me feel better about myself, but that was not the case. Our drug addiction was now public knowledge, and Ronald and I were the topic of discussion among many church members. When I walked into the church building, I sensed the judgment and gossip that was constantly whirling around. People didn't really know what to say to me, so they didn't say anything. Even in the midst of my church family, I felt alone.

Malinda made an unsuccessful attempt to reunite with the father of her children, but the results were disastrous. Right after I gave her a money order for my share of the rent, she got into a huge fight with her husband and in a fit of rage, left her purse sitting on the bus stop. Up to that point, Mr. Segura had been patient with us, allowing us to make two monthly rent payments. We were already behind when she lost the money orders, and he lost his patience. We both had to find another place to live.

I reached out to Grandma Essie for help. After having raised her children and grandchildren, she didn't have the energy for her great-grandchildren, but she was instrumental in finding us another place to live. Cousin Artis, a ninety-six-year-old retired doctor, had an empty rental unit in the back of his house on Denker Avenue near Slauson. Grandma Essie arranged for us to stay there for three hundred dollars a month. I was excited and relieved that, for the first time, I would have a place of my own. But there was a part of me that dreaded the thought of living alone. I remembered thinking that if I sent Ronald away the addiction would go with him, but that was not the case. Even with my uncertainties, I was still excited and hopeful about my newfound independence.

Cousin Artis' place came completely furnished so I only had to take my babies and all of our clothes. My days were spent in a constant dichotomy: happy to be sober again, but afraid that it wouldn't last, relieved to be in my own space, but fearful that I wouldn't be able to handle living alone. Ronald was released from the county jail nine days after my father's funeral. I expected him to be with me to help me with the boys, but he had other plans. He continued living with his girlfriend, leaving me alone to contend daily with my inner demons. He would visit once or twice each week with a little money for diapers and milk, and to hug and kiss his sons, but each time he went home to his other woman. He left me steeping in a stew of emotions; anger, pain, resentment, and guilt; all of which became a recipe for disaster.

The next few months proved to be some of the darkest days of my entire life. Fully enslaved by my addiction, I didn't recognize the person I had become. In a chaotic free-fall, I cried out for help and this time my older brother, Andrew, provided me with a soft place to land. My mother was always there for me, but I was so tired of myself that I assumed there might be a part of her that was tired of me as well. Andrew had only a one-bedroom apartment, but he allowed me to convert his dining room area into a bedroom.

It was a very small space, just big enough for a day bed. I slept on the top and my babies slept on the bottom, which gave me the perfect vantage point from which to watch them sleep, breathe and dream. I would stare at them for hours, wondering what kind of people they would grow up to be. I'd imagine that we were living in a home overlooking the ocean, with a swimming pool in the back yard, and that we didn't have a care in the world. The only time I felt fully content and at peace was when I blocked out the reality of my circumstances and focused on my three, beautiful babies. I had a very strong feeling inside that things would only get better with time.

Living with Andrew was added incentive for me to avoid getting high. The shame of being addicted was too great to let my big brother see that side of me. For most of my life, he had been my defender, protector, and counselor. When I was only eight years old, he beat up a little boy for breaking my ukulele. And when I was in the fifth grade, he walked me to school to scare off some bullies who had threatened to beat me up.

"You're cute Jackie! Don't chase boys, let them chase you!" I was thirteen years old when he gave me this advice. Just like my mother, I thought he was only saying that because he was my brother and he loved me. Andrew was one of my biggest supporters, instrumental in laying the foundation for my career. He introduced me to my mentor, Mr. Dunlap, as well as many of the artists I worked with including Andre Crouch, BeBe Winans, and Yolanda Adams. Along with my mother, Andrew always did his best to encourage me. He even allowed me to drive his 1976, red convertible Cadillac when he wasn't using it.

The first month in my brother's home was like a recovery period for me. I needed to get over the series of binges that I engaged in while living with cousin Artis. During that time, I reached such a low point that I even considered suicide. I didn't really want to die, I simply wanted to be sober and normal, and I was able to find that place with my brother.

Just as I began to settle into an almost blissful routine of caring for my babies, working out, and going to church, Andrew and I received a call from my Aunt Malinda. Once again, she and her five children had no place to go and asked if he would be willing to open his doors to them, and he reluctantly said yes. Malinda slept on the couch and all of her children slept on the floor. After a few weeks, however, it became clear that his one-bedroom apartment was not big enough for three adults and eight children—so I called my mother. She also had only a one-bedroom apartment, but she made room for my babies and me. I slept in the living room on the couch, and they slept on a makeshift mattress that I made out of pillows and blankets on the floor. The space was limited, but my mom provided us with an abundance of love, which was instrumental in my continued recovery.

I was offered a job as music teacher and director over the children's choir at the church that I attended since the age of fifteen. The church expanded to include a private charter school. The pay was minimal, but they allowed my sons to attend the pre-school for free. I wrote songs, arranged choral parts, taught vocal technique and basic music theory. I found a true sense of purpose in working with the children and doing what I did best. Also, getting the boys dressed in their uniforms and taking them to school every day made me feel like a normal, productive human being again. Drug addiction was now a thing of the past. I only wished I could have said the same for Ronald.

After he was released from the county jail, he came to visit us once as we celebrated Daniel's fourth birthday, then continued right where he left off before he was arrested. I didn't hear from him for several weeks. When I finally did, it was a collect call from a correctional facility.

AUNTIE LINDA

ANDREW GOUCHÉ

CHAPTER THREE

LITTLE GUYS

When I heard Ronald's voice on the phone, part of me felt relieved that it wasn't someone calling from the hospital or even worse, the morgue, telling me that something horrible had happened to him. The other part of me was disappointed and angry. I knew immediately that this time around he would be away much longer than his brief stint in the county jail, and the first thought in my mind was *divorce*. I wasn't willing to put my life on hold and wait for him. I wasn't surprised, however, that he was calling me from a correctional facility. I saw the direction he was headed in and knew that it would not end well. I devised a plan to go on with my life as a single mother.

"You know what this means, don't you?" I said in a matter-of-fact tone.

"Yes," he responded. I had threatened him with divorce many times and my words didn't come as a surprise to him.

"How are the boys?" He immediately switched the focus to the topic of our children. They were the only connection we had left, and even though I wouldn't have admitted it at that moment, that connection was strong enough to last for the rest of our lives.

"They're doing just fine. " As relieved as I was to finally hear from him, all of my responses were short and abrupt. The realization that I would have to visit him in prison to allow him to father our children filled me with anger and a pain to which I had already become accustomed. The first five years of our marriage consisted only of turmoil and trauma, with little sparks of bright light that broke through our cloud covering from time to time. The birth of each of our sons interrupted the distress of our addiction and gave us both a reason to keep fighting. Now, a new chapter had begun.

Having experienced two completely different personalities in Davion and Daniel, when little Sir first arrived, I didn't know what to expect from him. I wondered if he was going to be like Dave—a calm, quiet baby, or like Daniel, a demanding and intense little man-child. But he wasn't like either of his brothers. Sir Darryl was his own unique soul, a contemplator. He was neither easy nor demanding, but stubborn. As a newborn he was more like Dave, quiet for the most part. But when he became a toddler, I realized that he had been observing every situation and deciding how he wanted to deal with it.

Sir Darryl didn't want to do anything the way either of his brothers had done. He always wanted to do his own thing. My mother convinced me that two years was the diaper-cut-off age, and I had been successful at potty training both Davion and Daniel on, or shortly after their second birthday. Daniel was a breeze. As soon as he realized he could go in the pot and not on himself, he immediately changed his M.O. Because of him, I'd convinced myself that I was an expert potty trainer, but little Sir rewrote that narrative. His second birthday had come and gone, and he still wasn't quite ready to give up his right to *go* on his own terms. Because they were so close in age, there was a brief period when all three of them were in diapers at the same time, which was quite trying, so I was determined to bring that chapter to an end. Sir Darryl was well into his third year of life by the time he realized that he was fighting a losing battle, and the day of the diaper was over!

When they became toddlers, each of the boys tried their hand at throwing a tantrum. If there was one thing I did not believe in, it was tantrums. That was one of those parenting decisions I made long before I had children—I was never going to be the woman in the store trying verbally to convince her screaming child to calm down and get up off the floor while the other shoppers looked on in dismay. Each of my sons was allowed to throw exactly *one* tantrum. As soon as they did, by the time the palm of my hand was finished with their little thigh, they were convinced that throwing a fit was not something they would do a second time. Just because many people tend to go too far with physical discipline and cross over into the realm of abuse, doesn't mean that it should be completely eradicated. Of course, each child is unique and not all of them need to be physically corrected. But as a single mother with three rambunctious little boys, I knew how important it was for me to establish my authority over them early. It wasn't something I had to continually work on. I simply made sure they understood who was in charge. They were all fully convinced by the age of three.

Now that I understood what it meant to be a mom, I had a much greater appreciation for my mother. One of the things I appreciated about her most was that she always expressed her love for me. There was never a shortage of hugs and kisses, or words of encouragement and praise. When I was younger, she often referred to me as her "pretty little baby girl" and she was always doting over me, sometimes to the point of annoyance. But deep down inside, I was grateful to know that someone genuinely loved and cared for me that way. I had never taken a psychology class or studied the importance of positive physical and verbal interaction with young children. But I knew how nourishing my mother's love was to me, and I was determined to nourish my children in the same way. I knew exactly how my mother felt. Those three little men had taken ownership of my heart. I now understood the *lay-down-your-life* kind of love!

Even though I had three children of my own, the love that my mother had for me when I was a little girl had not changed. If anything, it had intensified. She had enough room in her heart and her home for me, and my three babies. It didn't matter how small her place was, she always made room for us. It didn't matter how little food she had, she was always willing and able to stretch it so that we all had enough to eat. In the process of overcoming my addiction, she was the one who held my hand and walked with me to sobriety. Betty Gouché was my angel. For the first year after Ronald was locked up again, I was honest with myself and with my mother. Having any amount of money would trigger the cravings, and I knew that I was incapable of handling them by myself. So, on the first and fifteenth of each month, my mother went with me to cash my check and shop for our necessities. Whatever money was left, she would handle for me.

After being sober for just about a year, things began to change drastically. As my environment changed, my perspective changed, my view of myself changed. I no longer saw myself as a drug addict and welfare mother. Even though I was still dependent on the checks I received each month, I knew I was greater than my circumstances.

When I looked in the mirror, I was more and more pleased with what I saw. I began to receive regular calls for background vocal sessions, which would have supplemented my welfare income beautifully. The problem was that we were expected to report all sources of income to the county. At first, I would report everything I earned because I wanted to be honest and ethical. But every dime that I reported would be deducted from my check, so I ended up with the same amount of money, $850 a month, plus food stamps. Nothing about that made sense to me. How was I supposed to provide a decent life for my children on less than a thousand dollars a month? For a while, I stopped reporting my extra income, but I didn't feel good about that.

My relationship with God had grown to the point where we had an open line of communication daily. I would pray, attend church, give offerings, and always try my best to do what I thought was the right thing. Even during my struggles, I enjoyed a consistent flow of blessings and peace that could not be bought with money.

I needed to figure out a way to solve my dilemma. Would I continue to lie in order to receive a welfare check? Or would I have faith and trust God to provide for me? So many times, I felt the prompting to simply stop filling out the form and let go of the county check, but I didn't have a consistent source of income. The background sessions were sporadic, but I needed something I could count on. On the weekends, I would hang out, and perform regularly at a club in Hollywood called *Singers* where I was able to connect with more people in the music industry. My background vocal sessions increased steadily, and I was no longer comfortable relying on welfare.

In December of 1988, I filled out my last CA7 reporting form and believed with all my heart that God would provide for me. It's funny how faith works. Within a few days, I received a phone call from a producer/songwriter that I'd met at the club. He asked if I would be interested in singing twenty demos for him and offered me $100/song. I was able to earn $2000 within two weeks. My faith had been instantly rewarded. This pattern continued for a few months and my income had grown way beyond the eight hundred fifty dollars I had been getting from the county. There were times, however, when things were a bit scarce and I became slightly anxious, wondering if I would be able to make ends meet. But whenever that happened, God always came through.

In March of 1989 something wonderful and unexpected happened. An old friend from the Young Americans named LueCinda Ramseur called and invited me to be a part of a group she was putting together to audition for an M&M's candy television commercial. This would be the first time I was hired to be on camera, everything I had done in my career up to that point was some form of audio recording or live stage performance. Seven groups were auditioning that day, with lots of familiar faces in each group. The competition was brutal, and the voices were amazing, but it was our group that was ultimately chosen.

The pay was much higher than anything I had ever earned, over two thousand dollars for the initial session, and an additional ten thousand dollars in residuals the next year. This money was more than enough to make up for the welfare check I had given up. The most beautiful part was that, unlike the payment for *The Color Purple* session, this money did not come with any cravings. I knew when I deposited that check that my days of addiction were truly a thing of the past.

My mom was playing piano for Mt. Olive Second Baptist, the church we had attended when I was a little girl. In addition to the commercial, studio sessions, and live gigs I was already doing, she was able to get me a regular job working with the youth choir. It was only a small amount of money, one hundred and twenty-five dollars each Sunday. But it was nice to be able to work only on Sundays, allowing me to remain free to travel and do sessions during the week. Each week I dressed my three little soldiers, often in the same outfit, took them to church, and set them on the front row by the piano, where they usually slept through the entire service.

Ron Ron was fourteen years old at the time and he was learning to play the drums. He had been playing at his great-grandmother's church, but I convinced him that playing with me would be more fun. I also offered to pay him thirty-five dollars each Sunday. He quickly accepted my offer, said goodbye to Grandma Essie's church, and joined me in this musical endeavor. Even though it was only one day each week, having him with me on Sundays gave me great joy.

Ron Ron lived with great-grandma Essie, in the same house for his entire childhood. When Ronald and I got married, he and Essie decided it was best for Ron Ron to continue living with his great-grandmother because they didn't want to uproot him. They wanted him to have a sense of stability.

~

My mother continued to babysit for me whenever I worked. It was comforting to know that the same woman who had cared for me all my life was now caring for my children. I was confident that they were in good hands. It was interesting, however, to see the difference in our parenting styles, and how the boys responded. When I was a child, my mother was not nearly as strict as her parents had been with her, but she still ruled with a pretty firm hand. That same hand did not seem to be as effective with my boys—especially Daniel. Talking was one of his favorite pastimes. He was always either asking us how the world worked or telling us how he thought it should work.

One day, we were all sitting at the dinner table for a family meal, and Daniel had a lot that he wanted to share. My mom, having been raised in a different generation, told him to be quiet and eat his food. Daniel thought about what she said, and after about ten seconds, decided that he had something else he needed to say. My mother, in a more forceful tone, said to him,

"Daniel, I said be quiet and eat your food!" He paused for another ten or fifteen seconds and began talking again.

"Shut up Daniel!" my mother yelled. At this point, I was concerned for my baby, as I felt the sting of the moment. But he did not possess the fear that I had developed under my mom's firm hand. All he knew was, just like the playpen, he didn't understand the concept of "*shut-up.*" After another ten to fifteen seconds of silence, Daniel wrinkled his eyebrows, and the next thing that came out of my three-year-old baby's mouth was "*I gotta talk!*"

His words cut through the tension in the air like a knife, and everyone at the table, including my mother, broke out in laughter. I was tickled and intrigued with the courage and determination of this little guy, and his defiance of his grandmother's commands. When I was young, that would have been considered "talking back" to my mother, something that we just didn't do. And if she had fixed her mouth to say something like that to her parents, she would certainly have gotten knocked to the other side of the room. But Daniel didn't know that kind of fear. He had a mind of his own and, in his mind, as long as he had something to say, he felt he should have the right to say it.

Before they were even able to form words, I taught my babies their ABCs. They all knew how to read long before they began attending school. Even though I had not finished college, I understood the importance of education and I was determined to give my boys a solid foundation, both academically and musically. When I wasn't teaching them reading, writing, or arithmetic, I was teaching them the definition of pitch, sharp, flat, and interval. I showed them how to find middle-C on the piano, and how to play a C major scale before their little fingers were barely long enough to stretch over the keys. They knew the difference between the treble and bass clef, and they knew the lines and spaces on the staff as well as their ABCs. I explained to them not only how to hear a note, but also to visualize it, and then recreate it accurately with their voice.

Davion was especially interested in singing. He was only five years old when he sang his first solo in church.

"Oh holy night, the stars are brightly shiiiiiiiiiiiiiiiiii-ning! It is the night of our dear Savior's birth . . ." The first syllable in the word shining was Davion's favorite part of the song. It was only supposed to be held for two beats, but he always held on to it until *he* felt like letting it go. The most amazing part about that five-year-old singing *Oh Holy Night* was the accuracy with which he hit each note. I knew as I taught him the song that his voice was special, but no one could have told me then just how special it would be.

We had been living with my mother in her one-bedroom apartment for nearly two years when she was informed that they were going to raise her rent. They told her that she had to pay an additional $500 a month because of the number of people that lived there. Even though I was earning a decent amount of money, it didn't make sense to pay that much more for such a small apartment. I was the reason they raised my mom's rent, but she never made me feel bad for it.

"I guess that means we'll just have to find another place to live," she said with simple resolve. Just about the time when we began our search for another apartment, I received a phone call from another old friend named Debbie McClendon-Smith. She asked if I would be interested in leading Praise & Worship, filling in for another mutual friend. He was working as the Minister of Music for an amazing woman pastor named Beverly "Bam" Crawford, and he needed someone to step in when he had a Sunday gig. I wasn't quite sure what she meant by the phrase Praise & Worship, but I knew it had something to do with playing and singing in church, and I was confident that it was something I could handle. My mother and I attended the church service the very next Sunday to see exactly what I would be expected to do.

Pastor Bam's service began at 8 a.m. and our church didn't start until eleven a.m., so we were able to attend both. The church service we experienced that day was unlike any other. Pastor Bam Crawford was different from any other pastor. Not only was she the first woman I'd ever seen in the pulpit, but she also taught the Bible more thoroughly than any man I'd ever heard. I had spent most of my childhood in church and was familiar with many of the stories from the Bible. I knew all about Adam and Eve, Abraham, Isaac, Jacob, and the Children of Israel. I was well acquainted with Noah, Sampson and Delilah, Daniel in the lion's den, Jonah in the belly of the whale, the three Hebrew boys in the fiery furnace, the Prodigal Son, and, of course, Jesus on the cross. As much preaching as I'd been exposed to, I had never really heard "*teaching*," until that Sunday.

I received a call from Pastor Bam's secretary to set up a meeting. Even though I was extremely nervous, the meeting went very well.

"Tell me about yourself," she said in a matter-of-fact tone. After seeing her in the pulpit the previous Sunday, I felt so thoroughly intimidated that I hardly knew where to begin. So, I just took a deep breath and started spilling my guts.

"Well, I'm married, but my husband is incarcerated. We were both addicted to crack cocaine, but I've been sober for just over a year." I don't know why I started with the worst of me, but her response was quite comforting.

"A year of sobriety is wonderful!" She paused for a moment. "Go on," she said, apparently interested in the rest of my story.

"I have three baby boys. They are three, four, and five years old."

"Wow, you've been busy!" We both laughed. By this time, I felt at ease and shared with her many other details about my life, including my experience as a PTL singer and a background vocalist for Andre Crouch.

The very next Sunday, I filled in for the worship leader and, from that day on, I had a feeling that my life would never be the same. After stepping in for him twice within a few weeks, he quit working for the church, and I was hired as his full-time replacement. I was not surprised when I received the call. Something inside had already assured me that the job was mine.

The money from the M&M's commercial had just about dried up, and the job at the church was exactly what I needed to provide me with a regular income and a sense of stability. It was awesome to be able to receive a weekly check for doing what I loved to do; sing and play the piano. It was considerably more than I received from the other church. For a while, I tried to do both jobs, but I wasn't always able to make it on time to Mt. Olive, so I eventually quit. Another benefit of working for Pastor Bam was that hearing her teach each Sunday caused me to grow spiritually.

Having a job with a steady income made it easy for us to qualify for our new apartment. We found a place in the city of Paramount and moved in the very next month. I immediately enrolled Davion and Daniel in school, even before unpacking the boxes.

My mother, my younger brother, my three sons, and I were all living together in a two-bedroom apartment. It was a little bigger than the place we moved from, but it was still a tight squeeze. After living there for only a few months, my mother found a job as an apartment manager in a place right around the corner. We moved again to the building on Gundry Avenue, where we no longer needed to live together. My mom lived rent-free as the property manager, and I rented the apartment directly across the hall from hers. This made it quite convenient for her to care for the boys while I worked. On the rare occasions when my mother was unavailable, or just too tired to deal with three little guys, I would call one of Ronald's sisters.

AUNTIE RENNIE

Ronald has three sisters and one brother. The sister in the middle of the three girls is Arthurine, but everyone calls her Rennie. She is the most eclectic of the bunch; a warm, beautiful, happy soul who dances to her own tune. She never had children of her own, but she was like a mother-buddy-playmate to her nieces and nephews, all of whom love her dearly. Rennie would often come to pick the boys up and take them to the beach or the park, or just come over and hang out with us. Because of her passion for photography she enjoyed taking pictures of the children, dressing them in creative costumes like African warriors or cowboys. She was the only one of Ronald's sisters with whom I developed a real relationship when the boys were young, and the only other person besides my mom and my Aunt Malinda that I trusted to watch my sons. The problem with Rennie was that she shared her brother's addiction, which I had to learn the hard way.

One day I got a call from Scott Smith to do a background vocal session in Orange County, about an hour from where we lived. I knew I would be gone for a long time and although my mother was always willing to babysit, the boys could sometimes be a handful. I didn't want to burden her with keeping them for the entire day. So, I called Auntie Rennie and asked if she would ride with me to the session and keep my sons and my car while I worked. She gladly accepted. The plan was for her to take them to a nearby park, and then feed them before picking me up from the studio at five o'clock. But when the clock struck five, Rennie was nowhere to be found. At first, I wasn't concerned. I figured she and the boys were having fun and had just lost track of time.

Another thirty minutes passed and still, no Rennie. At this point, I was a bit concerned. I knew my instructions were clear and I made sure she had the address. But I also knew that Rennie was a free spirit and not usually bound by rules or clocks. I made the conscious decision to take a few deep breaths and not to worry. I was a bit embarrassed because the session was over, and the producer and the owner of the studio were waiting with me until my ride showed up.

"I'm sure she'll be here soon. She has my children with her."
Another thirty minutes passed and still, no Rennie. I could feel my
temperature rising. It was six o'clock, a full hour past the time that she
was supposed to pick me up. What could possibly have happened? Were
they in a car accident? Were my sons okay? Was Rennie okay? There
were no cell phones or pagers, and I had no way of reaching her. At this
point, I began to worry.

"Do you want me to drive you home?" Scott offered. My embarrassment had turned to anxiety and fear. Where could she possibly be with
my babies? After a few more minutes I accepted Scott's offer to drive
me home. I apologized for the inconvenience, but I was more concerned about Rennie and the boys.

During the ride home, Scott first attempted to assure me that
everything would be okay, and then he tried to make small talk. I don't
remember a word he said because of the mayhem that was going on
inside my head. I appeared to be okay on the outside, but on the inside,
I felt like a volcano getting ready to erupt. I was hoping to find Rennie
and the boys waiting for us when we finally arrived home, but there was
no such luck.

As soon as I walked in the door, my mother could see the panic on
my face.

"What's wrong?" She asked.

"Rennie never showed up," I said, choking on the lump in my
throat.

"What do you mean, she never showed up," my mother's brow
wrinkled in confusion.

"Rennie dropped me off at the studio and took my car and the boys. She was supposed to come back and get me at five o'clock, but she never showed up!"

Both of us were dumbfounded. We tried calling the police to report them missing but only found that it had not been long enough for us to make a report. I tried calling hospitals to see if they'd been in an accident, but that didn't yield any results either. More than three hours had passed without me knowing the whereabouts of my babies and at this point, I was beginning to lose it. The intensity of the fear, frustration, anger, and anxiety was matched only by the deep, penetrating love I had for my babies, and not knowing their whereabouts was killing me.

I called Grandma Essie only to find that she had not heard from Rennie. I called Ronald's mother, Mattie, but she wasn't there either. Images of my son's bodies, mangled by the metal from the car flashed through my mind, but instead of allowing those thoughts to take over, I called my aunt Malinda and asked her to pray.

"The devil is a liar!! He cannot put his hands on those boys!" She went straight into prayer warrior mode.

"Don't you worry Jackie, they are fine. Nothing is going to happen to them! You have to trust that God is taking care of them, wherever they are!" I'd seen God answer Malinda's prayers on many occasions, and I had no choice but to believe He would do the same thing in this situation.

I had figured out that Rennie was probably somewhere getting high, but I could not wrap my mind around the fact that she was doing it while my sons were with her. I remembered what it felt like to be deep in the throes of addiction, so I understood how she could fail to pick me up. What I could not understand was how Rennie could stay gone so long. She had no children of her own, so she couldn't possibly know exactly what she was putting me through.

Four hours passed, then five, still no Rennie. I went from praying and telling myself not to worry, to cursing Rennie and screaming at the top of my lungs. Then, I simply fell to my knees in front of the couch and sobbed, soaking the pillows until they dripped through to the floor.

When midnight came and I still hadn't heard from her, I realized that my only real option was to calm myself down and wait. I had called everyone I could think of, I'd prayed every prayer I knew, I'd uttered every profane word in my vocabulary, and I'd cried until there were no tears left. Drained of every ounce of energy, I finally fell asleep around four in the morning. But at eight in the morning my eyes popped open, and I remembered that my sons were still missing. What made it even worse was that she still had my car, so I couldn't even go and look for them. Then, at around eight-thirty, the phone rang. It was Grandma Essie.

"Jackie, Rennie dropped your boys off and gave me the keys to your car. She said you were coming to pick them up." There was no real urgency in her voice, so I knew right away that they were all right. The relief I felt was as much physical as it was emotional. It felt as if I had been choking all night and now I could breathe freely.

"Give me about thirty minutes." I needed a ride from Paramount to Inglewood, so I immediately knocked on my neighbor's door and offered them $20 to drive me to pick up my boys. Still wearing my clothes from the day before, we were in the car and on our way to Grandma Essie's within minutes.

When we arrived, the boys were asleep on the sofa and chair in the living room. I picked them up one by one and held on to them until I felt the stress of the previous day begin to melt away. They had spent most of the night in the car and were still very tired, but generally okay. They were only four, five, and six and didn't even realize that something had gone wrong. All they knew was that they had fun at the park for several hours, ate dinner, and slept in the car. I was so angry with Rennie that I didn't want to see her face or hear her name for at least a year. I eventually forgave her, but Rennie was so ashamed that she didn't want to come around me even when she was invited.

AUNTIE REENIE

CHAPTER FOUR

STABILITY & SERENDIPITY

Living in my own apartment felt incredible. God had blessed me to get off of welfare and earn enough money to pay rent and provide for my children. I went to Grandma Essie and asked if Ron Ron could come and live with us but, once again, she and his aunts decided that it would be best for him to stay with her. I was heartbroken. I wanted the boys to be raised with their big brother, but it was out of my hands. He would come and visit often, and the boys were always excited to spend time with him. "You know what this means, don't you?" I said in a matter-of-fact tone.

Our apartments were on the second floor, with patios overlooking the playground, so it was easy for us to keep an eye on the boys while they played for hours. My little brother, Richard, who is five years older than Davion, took on the role of their tor-mentor. He forced them to fight with some of the neighborhood kids, making sure that they never backed down. From "let's see how far you can throw the ball" to "who can beat up who," Richard constantly presented them with challenges, seeing to it that they developed into strong, fearless young men who were always able to hold their own. Of course, he didn't realize the importance of what he was doing. He was simply being himself and playing with his nephews. Unaware of the fights at the time, I found out about my little brother's antics years later. It's a good thing I didn't know because it kept me from interfering with the process of making my sons the resilient, strong, fearless young men that they would eventually become.

Ron Ron was also instrumental in helping develop the fighter instincts in his little brothers. When he wasn't teaching them to play Street Fighter, Tekken, or Mortal Kombat, he was strapping the man-sized boxing gloves on their tiny hands and making them fight one another. I'm not sure if it is innate, or if it's something that they developed under the tutelage of their big brother and uncle, but all three of my sons have an extremely competitive edge. If one learned something, they all learned it. And there was a never-ending debate about who was better at it.

Although Sir Darryl was the youngest, Daniel was the smallest of his brothers. Sir's hefty appetite as a baby allowed him to make up for being a tiny little preemie. He began to outgrow Daniel by the time he reached the age of three. But Daniel's size was by no means a handicap. If anything, his small stature motivated him to show everyone just how tough he was. Daniel had not even made it through the first day in his new second-grade class when I received a phone call from the principal asking me to come to the school. Daniel had beat up one of his classmates and was being sent home for fighting.

I was neither surprised nor angry that Daniel beat the little boy up. Besides teaching them how to read, write, sing and play the piano,

I taught them never to fight against their brother, only for or with them. I taught them never to hit a girl, regardless of what she did. Always walk away from a confrontation with a girl, no matter how crazy she decided to act. Most importantly, I taught them never to allow anyone to bully them. I told them that if someone ever hit them, or even threatened to hit them, they had every right to beat that person up. I even encouraged them to make sure they came out of the fight as the winner.

I realize that my advice may not have been politically correct. I probably should have taught them conflict resolution, or to turn the other cheek, but I was often bullied as a child. As a non-confrontational introvert, I didn't learn to stand up for myself until well into adulthood. Also, having been known as the smart girl in most of my classes sometimes caused trouble. In the third grade, Donna Franklin punched me in the stomach because I wouldn't give her answers to the test. I called on my Aunt Malinda to defend me because I just wasn't a fighter, which is precisely why I made sure that my sons were!

When I arrived at the school, I had to put on my "angry mother" hat for the principal. He expected me to be appalled at my son's behavior, so I played the role.

"Now Daniel, you know you're not supposed to go around hitting people," I said,

"But mommy, you told me to . . ." I cut him off before he could finish his sentence.

"No more hitting! Do you understand me?"

I felt bad for being such a hypocrite, but I didn't want the principal to know that I was the reason the little boy got beat up. As soon as we got in the car I asked Daniel what happened.

"He stomped in a puddle and splashed water on me! And he did it on purpose. He started pointing at me and laughing, and all the other kids were laughing at me too. So, I punched him in his stomach as hard as I could!" I tried to hide my laughter, but I was truly proud of my little guy.

"That's right baby! You did the right thing."

"But you said no more hitting," he said in a puzzled tone.

"I only said that because that's what the principal wanted to hear. But if that boy does something like that again, you do exactly what you did!"

"He won't do it again," Daniel said with confidence. I was tickled by his certainty. A problem had arisen, and he knew just how to handle it.

In elementary school, all three of my boys got into fights from time to time, but Daniel fought much more than his brothers. When his classmates found out that his father was in prison, they would sometimes tease him about it. Daniel had a huge chip on his shoulder about his dad. He would dare someone to say something bad about his daddy, and when they did, he made sure they regretted it. Davion and Sir Darryl, on the other hand, were not nearly as sensitive about their father as Daniel was. But they were always willing to jump in the fight and defend their brother, even when he was the one who started it.

Being a single parent had its challenges, but the joy I found in mothering those three little men always outweighed the difficulties. There was something extremely special about having been the vessel through which those three exceptional beings came into the world. I was often overcome with sadness when I thought about all the memorable moments that Ronald was missing out on. Getting their first teeth; then losing them, learning to ride a bike without training wheels or making the honor roll, being selected as student of the month or winning first place in a spelling bee. Ronald was not there to witness many of the little milestones each of our sons reached, and that made my heart heavy.

Every night before going to bed we held hands and prayed. The boys would take turns leading the prayer, but no matter which one was leading it, each prayer contained the same requests.

"Lord, I thank you for this day, thank you for waking us up this morning and starting us on our way. Please bless my mommy, daddy, Bambama, Ron Ron and Uncle Richard, Grandma Mattie and Grandma Essie." Then they would all end the prayer with the same words, "and thank you Lord for bringing my daddy home from jail, in Jesus' name, Amen." For the first couple of years, I would hold my tears in until I had put the boys to bed and made it to my bedroom. Then I would grab a towel on my way to bed to keep from soaking my pillow with tears. As time went on, I developed a strength that I didn't realize I had. I eventually reached the point where I made it through the night without crying.

Daniel may have been sensitive about his father being in prison, but Ron Ron is the son that suffered the most as a result of his dad's absence. Ronald was incarcerated for Ron Ron's last two years of middle school. He was released, but it was only a couple of months before he was arrested again. For the entire four years that Ron Ron was in high school, Ronald was locked up. Ronald and I would talk on the phone several times each week, and he asked me to be sure to attend Ron Ron's graduation to represent him in his absence. Ron Ron's grades were exceptional, and Ronald wanted him to know that he was proud of him, even though he couldn't be there to tell him so. I had so many mixed emotions, including anger at Ronald for not being there for all of us, but especially for Ron Ron. I lamented the fact that I had not been allowed to be more involved in his childhood. When his father and I first got married, he was only ten, and I adored him. We had a few memorable moments together, but addiction and the difficulties of my marriage to his dad kept me from becoming the mother I would like to have been to him.

Working hard to take care of my little ones kept me on the go. Before I knew it, their big brother was a young man—with an absent father. Ron Ron always kept a smile on his face, no matter what was going on inside. On the day of his graduation, Ron Ron had several reasons to be filled with excitement and joy. His grandmother bought him a white, 1983 Ford Mustang for graduation and he and his friends were having a good time. His Aunt Rennie, Grandma Essie and I enjoyed watching them celebrate. After all the names were called and we came together again for hugs and pictures, I hugged him, and told him how proud I was of him. As we embraced, I whispered in his ear, "Your father is proud of you too." I was already fighting tears, but I had no idea the effect my words would have on him. Up to that moment, he was happy, laughing, and enjoying the day. But before I could finish my sentence, he buckled over and broke down in tears as if someone had punched him in the stomach. As I held Ron Ron in my arms, the tears that I had been holding back began to flow freely. When I let him go, he leaned over on his new Mustang and continued to cry. I felt horrible for having caused such an eruption of pain. I had been so consumed with my own issues with Ronald that I was somewhat disconnected from Ron Ron's experience of growing up without his father. He never expressed his disappointment, and always seemed to hold his pain inside. But today was different. We all stood by and watched as he let the tears flow. Nearly thirty minutes passed before he was finally able to shake it off and seemingly enjoy the rest of the day.

Ron Ron was no longer playing drums with me, but he was old enough to decide where he wanted to go on Sundays. He chose to continue going to church with me at Bible Enrichment. Inspired by a popular group called the *Gospel Gangstaz*, he even put together a rap group of his own called *KPS*, which stood for *Kings, Priests and Soldiers*. Ron Ron was gifted in many areas. He was a whiz at math and possessed a sense of humor and wit that made him fun to be around. He also had a natural swag that made his younger brothers want to be like him. KPS performed at the church at least once each month and they were a big hit.

"To God be the glory let the story be told, to him all praises owed and all blessings bestowed to me a young priest, just and upright. Walking by faith, not by sight, I'm real tight with God! They ain't believing all the blessings I'm receiving, standing strong in the Word, seeing demons retreating. My beliefs give me relief when dismayed, disarrayed, got on my knees, prayed! He laid his life down for us. That's why I'm glad to bust in his name no longer the same, I've been changed, rearranged my thought process and now I'm blessed, no longer contributing to the mess. Confess your sins and be acquitted, I know it's real because I did it. So if you coming along then get with it. Committed to the one on high, and if you don't know why then it's because you haven't given him a try . . ."

Ron Ron had become somewhat of a celebrity within the church and all of the young members were KPS fans, especially Davion, Daniel, and Sir Darryl. They knew all of the lyrics to every song and took great pride in the fact that Ron Ron was their older brother. Nearly everyone in the congregation, both young and old eagerly anticipated each fourth Sunday; youth Sunday, when they would get to see them perform.

Taking the boys to church on Sundays was as much a part of our lives as sending them to school Monday through Friday. Being a member of a spiritual community helped to stabilize me in many ways. Not only was I receiving a regular paycheck, but I also met some new friends who eventually became an instrumental part of raising my sons. Both La Renee and Stella became my best friend at the same time, but they were also like oil and water. As well as I got along with each of them, they did not get along with one another. At the time it was frustrating and somewhat difficult to manage. But in hindsight, I can see how they each played their own unique role in the lives of my children. Rena was a bit more of a tomboy than I was. She taught me how to shoot a jumper and a lay-up. She was always willing to go with me to take the boys to the park and play basketball—something I probably wouldn't have done alone. Rena was raising her nephew, Tony, who was the same age as Sir Darryl. Tony and Sir became the best of friends and remain friends to this day.

While Rena was my *"hang out and play with the boys"* friend, my relationship with Stella was on a completely different page. She was a gifted soprano and we worked together at the church. We also wrote songs together and I brought her in on some of my background vocal sessions. In 1992, she became pregnant and, after a few months, was no longer able to work on her job because it required her to be on her feet all day. We decided to get an apartment together where she could stay home and take care of the boys while I worked. We found a three-bedroom unit in a place called *The Park Apartments* in the city of Lakewood. It was perfect for us because of the swimming pool, playground, and affordable rent. The best part was that there was a gate on the south side of the complex that led directly to the campus of the elementary school. It almost seemed too good to be true.

The arrangement between Stella and I was like a perfect marriage—without the sex! I paid two-thirds of the rent and bills, and she was able to contribute in ways that were much more valuable than money. Not only did she cook, but she also made sure the meals were healthy and balanced. She kept the apartment clean, and with the help of the boys, she did the laundry. Stella always gave them responsibilities around the house and kept them accountable. She taught them how to be diligent, never to compromise their values, and made sure they understood the importance of having a good work ethic. She also taught them the meaning of the word articulate. Stella was a stickler about many things, which at times may have been a bit annoying. But the lessons they learned from her helped shape them into the responsible men they are today.

I began giving my sons piano lessons at the same time, but Daniel was the only one I didn't have to beg to spend time practicing. It was just the opposite. I had to coerce him into relinquishing the piano bench so one of his brothers could have a turn, neither of whom were as excited about playing the piano as Daniel was. Sir Darryl didn't seem to be interested in music at all. I had to practically force him to pay attention during our lessons. It didn't matter to me that he wasn't a willing participant. I was determined to teach him whether he wanted to learn or not. Then, when he was older, he would be able to choose how he would use the information rather than wishing he had learned it.

Sir Darryl always preferred playing outside with his friends to music lessons, but there was a point at which he stopped resisting. It wasn't until years later that I realized he always loved it, he just didn't like the idea of being made to do anything his brothers did. Despite his objections, I wasn't the type of mother to allow my children to decide for themselves what they wanted to do. My mother gave me a choice when I was seven, and I later regretted the choice that I made. I wasn't going to make that mistake with my sons. One of the keys to good parenting is using your wisdom and experience as an adult to make the best choices for your children until they are mature enough to choose for themselves.

Living in *The Park Apartments* was a time of extreme growth and stabilization. Andre and Sandra Crouch continued to hire me for background vocal sessions, which snowballed into a consistent flow of work.

Between 1985 and 1995, besides singing on *The Color Purple*, I had the pleasure of singing background on Quincy Jones's *Back on the Block* album as well as singing live behind him on the Johnny Carson show. I also performed live on Johnny Carson behind Diana Ross and Julio Iglesias. I was the alto voice of the background singers in the Tina Turner movie, *What's Love Got to Do With It* and appeared in an on-camera part in the movie *Two Can Play That Game*. I worked on the soundtrack for the movie *White Men Can't Jump*, and sang background for Patti LaBelle, Aaron Neville, Bobby Caldwell, Billy Joel, Sinead O'Conner, Irene Cara, Roy Orbison, Leonard Cohen, Ricky Martin, Dave Stewart, Chaka Kahn, Tina Turner, Stevie Wonder and, the most exciting session of all, Michael Jackson.

In early 1992, I was invited to go on a two-week trip to South Africa to sing behind Andre Crouch. I was extremely excited because this would be my first time traveling abroad. I immediately accepted the invitation, paid for my expedited passport, told my Pastor that I would be gone for two weeks, and was on my way. I didn't think twice about what would happen at church while I was gone. After the trip, I returned home expecting to simply step back into my position without a hitch, but that was not the case. When I showed up for rehearsal, another person was sitting at my keyboard, and I was informed that I would not be ministering the following Sunday.

A sudden shock went through my bones when I realized that I may have lost my job. How was I going to pay my rent? Or take care of my kids? I felt like the rug had been pulled from under my feet and I was back at square one. I showed up at church the following Sunday even though I wasn't leading worship. After church was over, Pastor Bam called me into her office.

"You are going to have to decide what's more important to you, your *career*, or your *ministry*," she said with certainty. Up until that time, I hadn't recognized or acknowledged the difference between the two. I needed to do some soul-searching, to take some time, and clearly define my roles. Undoubtedly, mother and provider were the two most vital ones. But when it came to my job and career, I had yet to decide exactly who I wanted to be, and how to become that woman. Did I see myself as a background singer or a worship leader, a musician or a minister? A few months later, I received an invitation that would force me to choose exactly who I was and what was most important to me. I was invited to go on a three-month tour to Japan, singing background for Stevie Wonder.

When I was in the seventh grade, I spent every evening listening to *Songs In The Key of Life*, learning every word to every song. Stevie Wonder's music introduced me to a whole new world and ignited within me the idea that I may one day add songwriter to my list of skills. The possibility of meeting and working with Stevie had only been a dream of mine since my middle school days. With the opportunity staring me in the face, I had to choose between living out that dream or staying home to take care of my boys and securing my position at the church.

I could not imagine turning down the chance to work with Stevie Wonder, so I accepted the job. We were scheduled to rehearse every night for two weeks before leaving for Japan. The first few nights of rehearsal, I was simply thrilled to be in the same room with him. But toward the end of the first week, I began to feel troubled. I tried my best to justify my decision and make myself believe that it was the right thing to do. The amount of money I would make with Stevie was five times what I was being paid at the church, but that was only for three months. After the tour was over, there were no guarantees. I also had to consider the fact that I would be away from my babies for that length of time.

The more I thought about the consequences of going on tour, the dream of working with my all-time favorite singer began to lose its luster. I was no longer at peace with my choice to accept the job, and I knew what I needed to do. But knowing it and doing it did not come with the same ease. I wrestled with myself and went to one more rehearsal. That night, it became crystal clear to me that I really had no business going on the road. My sons needed me to be there. My job needed me to be there.

As soon as I got home, I picked up the phone and called Nate, Stevie's musical director. I must have held the receiver in my hand for thirty minutes before actually dialing the number. I struggled to form the words to tell him that I was backing out of the gig. No matter how

I phrased it, it felt wrong. The Mother/Minister part of me was absolutely certain that I was doing the right thing. But the little girl from middle school singing *Ordinary Pain* until she couldn't keep her eyes open, she simply wanted to live out her dream.

"Hi Nate, it's Jackie." My heart was pounding.

"Hey Jackie, what's up?" After a moment of hesitation, I forced the words past the lump in my throat.

"I can't go."

"What do you mean, you can't go?" He said, angrily.

"I can't leave my children for three months. And if I go, I won't have a job when I get back." I expected more rebuttal or debate, but once I told him why I couldn't go, he simply wished me well.

"Alright then, you take care." I never heard from the Stevie Wonder camp again. Heartbroken that I came so close but was unable to actually share the stage with Stevie, I took comfort in knowing that I absolutely made the right choice. Within a few days, the pain of turning down my dream-gig began to subside and I, once again, found the greatest joy in sharing my gift with my boys.

I had been teaching them music for at least three years, and although it is possible for just about anyone to learn how to play an instrument, the ability to sing is a gift that can only be cultivated but never taught. My boys indeed had that gift. Many of the vocal exercises and techniques that I'd learned from Mr. Dunlap and from my experience with the Young Americans as a teen, I taught my children. One of my favorite ways to train their little ears was to have them sing a triad, then tell one or two of them to hold on to their note while instructing the other(s) to move in half or whole-step intervals either up or down. We would begin with a basic C major chord, move to a C sus, then F major, D minor, B flat major, G minor, E flat major, E diminished, E minor, and back to C. They had become so skilled at singing together that by the time they got in front of an audience it was second nature.

Christmas of 1992, at the ages of six, seven, and eight, the Farris brothers made their debut as a singing group. The congregation of our church was amazed to hear such intricate harmonies coming from those tiny bodies. They began with *God Rest Ye Merry Gentlemen*. Daniel sang the first solo, *"to save us all from Satan's power when we had gone astray . . . oh, tidings of comfort and joy, comfort and joy, oh tidings of comfort and joy"*. The second song in the medley was *Go Tell It On the Mountain*; Sir Darryl sang the solo on the verse, *"While shepherds kept their watching o'r silent flocks by night. Behold throughout the heavens, there shone a holy li–iiiiiight."* We ended with Davion leading *Oh Holy Night*. Although it was only a Christmas medley in church on a Sunday morning, I was as proud as if they had just performed at Carnegie Hall. They went on to sing with Andrae Crouch in a children's choir and appeared as musical guests on a local cable TV show. My babies sang every chance they got, and Daniel grew daily as a piano player, often performing classical pieces during youth service. Because of my position at the church, the platform was always available to them, and I used it as often as I could to help them sharpen their skills. Davion and Daniel relished every opportunity to sing or play. Little Sir, on the other hand, had to be persuaded, bribed, or threatened, but that didn't keep him from doing his absolute best when it was time to perform. Watching my babies shine whenever they were in front of an audience gave me the greatest joy, as well as a sense of accomplishment. It was clear that I was doing something right.

RICHARD WILLIAMS (MY BABY BROTHER)

CHAPTER FIVE

DADDY'S HOME

I remember sitting in the courtroom when the judge uttered the words "seventeen years." It was like we were both sentenced; Ronald to prison and me to a life of single motherhood. I added up the years and thought that our sons would be grown men by the time he came home. Ronald was intelligent enough to know that, in the process of the trial, his constitutional rights had been violated. So, he filed an appeal based on that fact.

It took a few years before anything significant happened. But in November of 1992, when the time came for the judge to decide on Ronald's case, he asked us to write character reference letters on his behalf. Though the boys were only in the first, second, and third grade, they were able to craft these letters in their own words, with their own little hands.

Sir Darryl's letter read:

> *Dear Judge Smith,*
>
> *My name is Darryl. I am in the first grade. I miss my daddy. I think three years is long enough. Please let him come home.*
>
> *Thank you.*

Daniel wrote:

> *Dear Judge Smith,*
>
> *I am writing this letter because I miss my dad. But I know he did something bad. But I know he won't do it again because he loves me. Please give him a chance.*
>
> *Thank you,*
>
> *Daniel Farris, 2nd grade.*

Davion's letter read:

> *Dear Judge Smith, my name is Davion Farris. My dad, Ronald Farris, has been in jail long enough. Will you please let him out? He really is a good man. He just needs a chance.*
>
> *Thank you! 3rd grade.*

I also wrote a letter to the judge. It reads:

> *Dear Judge Smith, I am writing simply to appeal to you on behalf of my husband, Ronald Farris. We have been married for almost nine years, five of which he's spent in prison. One of the reasons I continue to have hope in our life together is that I knew Ronald before his addiction to cocaine. He is an intelligent, loving and caring man. But the main reason that I continue to hope is that I know the God that is more powerful than any drug. And He was able to deliver me*

from that same habit, and cause me to go from welfare recipient, drug addict, to responsible, working mother. And I assure you He has made the same kind of change in Ronald. Judge Smith, all I ask of you is that you would not cause us to waste any more time in a penal system that really does nothing to rehabilitate its inmates, and allow us a chance, as soon as possible, to start rebuilding our family.
Thank you,
Mrs. Jacquelyn Farris

All of our letters were filed with the court on November 3, 1992. Three weeks later, Ronald was scheduled to appear in court again for the final judgment. We decided that, in addition to the letters, seeing Ron's wife and children sitting in the courtroom would positively impact the judge's decision. Although I wanted to be there to support him, I hated the feeling of the weight of the justice system. It pained me to know that the fate of our family was now in the hands of one man.

"Mr. Farris, have you waived your rights to a speedy trial?"

"Yes, your honor." It almost seemed as if his tongue was stuck to the roof of his mouth. I could tell he was terrified, even though he tried to keep a positive look on his face.

"The court, having accepted your of guilty, and with the agreement of the Los Angeles County District Attorney's office, is ready to pronounce sentence." My heart sank to the pit of my stomach as I remembered the last time we were in court, and Ronald was sentenced to seventeen years. I could barely breathe as the judge began to speak again.

"You have pled guilty to two counts of second-degree robbery." It wasn't often that I actually heard the charges against my husband.

When I did, the feeling was surreal, like someone was reading from a movie script.

"On both counts, the sentences will run concurrently. You are hereby sentenced to four years, plus a five-year prior prison term enhancement. Your total sentence therefore will be nine years." I wasn't sure whether to be relieved or crushed. It was less than the original seventeen years, but if he was going to remain locked up for another nine years, our children would still be adults by the time he came home.

"The court and the prosecution have agreed to award you three years and six months, time served." Ronald breathed a huge, audible sigh of relief. I knew then that it was good news. As the judge moved on to the next case; Ronald's attorney motioned to meet us in the hallway. He explained that Ron would only be required to serve half of his sentence, and with the three years' time served, we could already see the light at the end of the tunnel.

Exactly one year later, in the fall of 1993, Ronald was released from prison. He went directly to the halfway house where he was required to stay for a couple of months but was allowed to spend the weekends at home with us. It was a bit awkward for Stella when Ronald came home, so she and her newborn son, Alex, moved into a one-bedroom apartment within the same complex.

The day before he was released from the halfway house, we spent the entire day shopping, cooking, and decorating the apartment. The boys made a huge sign that read *WELCOME HOME DADDY!* We held a big party to celebrate his arrival and welcome him home. It was extremely emotional for me. I kept thinking about all the times the boys ended their prayer with *"thank you Lord for bringing our daddy home from jail."* God answered their prayers, and they were able to enjoy their father while they still called him *daddy*.

Ronald came home just in time to be there for their transition from being my baby boys to being young men. They were seven, eight, and nine years of age, and had not yet reached puberty. I was grateful that he arrived when he did because although I'd been able to handle my three little men up to this point, I felt ill-equipped to guide them through the next phase of their lives.

My sons had grown to the point where I needed to respect them as men. I took care in the way that I communicated with them, doing my best to be firm without yelling. I don't remember exactly where or how I had learned this, but I was aware that raising my voice at them would be counterproductive. Maybe it was because I was an only girl with three brothers, but I understood that there's something in a man's psyche that causes him to shut down when a woman is yelling at him. Whether it's his mother, wife, sister, or girlfriend, the effect of raising your voice at them is the same. They tune you out, and you lose a little bit of respect each time you do it. Every now and then, however, I had to remind my little men who was in charge. Whenever I struggled to get their attention, a nice long, firm pinch on the side was the perfect tool for the job.

As much as I enjoyed my boys, I often felt overwhelmed. Now that their father was home, I was ready to turn them over to him and enjoy a much-needed break. Ronald did not object at all. In fact, he loved the idea. We put our heads together and decided that it would be best for him to stay home and take care of the boys for a while before going back to work, giving them all a chance to get reacquainted, and me the opportunity to focus on my career. He had missed so many years with his sons, and they had missed their father. He spent the next year trying to make up for lost time, coaching flag football, little league baseball, and taking them to the batting cages and Karate lessons—all the things that I never would have even thought to do for them.

Living in Lakewood was no longer convenient because of the distance that I had to drive to get to work or a background vocal session, so we decided to move back to Los Angeles. We found a house for rent on 38th Place, between Arlington and Western Avenue. Now that his father was home and he was out of high school, Ron Ron decided to leave his great-grandmother's home on Park Circle and come live with us. Several years earlier, when the boys were small and their father was away, they often asked if they could have a puppy. My answer was always; "wait until your father comes home and we have a house with a yard." After moving into the house on 38th Place, we were finally able to get the boys the puppy they always wanted, a black, Chinese Chow Chow. Ronald had his wife, all four of his sons, and a puppy named Solomon under one roof and the picture was complete.

The boys took on the identities of *Leonardo, Donatello,* and *Michelangelo.* One of their friends would have to become *Raphael* when they came over to play. Teenage Mutant Ninja Turtles was a very popular cartoon series at this time, and when they weren't doing homework or chores, they were turtles. So, when Ronald told them that he was going to enroll them in Karate school, they nearly flipped their little shells. Their uncle Richard and big brother Ron Ron would take turns as Master Splinter, depending on who was available and willing to enter their fantasy world. Each of them had already groomed the boys to be fighters. Now, they were going to officially learn how to do it right.

Davion, Daniel, and Sir Darryl began attending Kajukenbo classes in the summer of 1995. Kajukenbo is a form of combat that combines Karate, Judo/jiujitsu, Kenpo, and boxing. They learned katas; a choreographed pattern of movements designed to develop muscle memory, like the scales of a pianist. They diligently practiced them every day. After several months of lessons, the instructors would choose two students and have them spar against one another, in preparation for the upcoming tournament. My sons were clearly the fiercest competitors in the school, so the instructors would usually pit them against a much bigger and stronger kid. It seemed unfair, but it was strategic. In the regional tournament, they don't choose opponents based on their size, but their age and their skill level. So it's not unusual for a student to fight someone much bigger. The three of them advanced quickly through the ranks. By the end of the year, they had all made it to the third level and earned their orange belt.

Davion recalls his experience fighting a kid named Nelson.

"We were both twelve years old, but I was around five feet tall, and Nelson was five feet, six inches. My classmates knew me as the kick master. Roundhouse, crescent, butterfly, front kick, I was skillful at them all. We were told to face one another, bow, and get in position. Sifu Darnell gave us the command with one single word,

'Fight!' Without hesitation, I immediately jumped up and kicked Nelson in the head!

'Point, Davion.' We lined up once again.

'Fight!' a second kick to the head!

'Whoooooooah!' the classmates roared. Nelson is steaming, two back-to-back kicks to the head. His eyes were red with anger. Round three,

'Fight!' convinced that a third kick would not be successful, I decided to try a reverse punch. Nelson blocked that punch so hard that he flung me off of my stance. It was at that moment that I realized the disparity in our upper-body strength. Nelson returned my reverse punch with a hefty reverse punch of his own. With every ounce of strength he could muster, beginning in his toes up through his calves, to his thighs, up his back, to his shoulders, to his arms, to my face, that punch lifted me completely up in the air, then slammed me to the floor. I could barely hear the roar of my classmates because of the ringing in my ears. Sifu Darnell stopped the fight."

The regional tournament was both exciting and frightening for me to watch. I knew my sons well enough to know that they were all great fighters, but it's just painful to watch someone hit or kick your child. My fear, however, did not last long. Ronald and I watched proudly as each one of our boys came out of their match as the victor. They all had an extremely intense sense of competition, insisting on being the best at whatever they did.

~

Living on one income was becoming increasingly difficult with the growing needs of our family. After a little over a year, we decided it was time for Ronald to get a job, which was also easier said than done, considering his record. Fortunately, someone was willing to overlook Ronald's past and offer him a job. Jackson Limousine was the number one, Black-owned limo service in Los Angeles, and the owner, E.J. Jackson was a warm-hearted, yet shrewd businessman. He served all the major Hollywood events and award shows and was very well known amongst celebrities. Ronald dove in head-first, becoming super-chauffeur, while maintaining his position as Wonder-Dad. He would get up at the crack of dawn, clean his car, stock it with goodies and be off to pick up his first client.

Even though he was no longer in his former field of electronics, Ronald was proud to go to work every day, and it showed in the excellence with which he served his clients. After work or on his days off, however, it was all about the boys. He started by becoming the coach for Sir Darryl's flag football team. Sir was excited to have his dad as the coach but was upset that he wasn't able to tackle anyone. Up until the time that their father came home, the boys' only experience with sports had been whatever games they played during recess in elementary school or playing basketball at Rowley Park with Rena and me. The reason Ronald started with football was because of the season. However, baseball was his first love.

As soon as football season was over, Ronald began preparing the boys for baseball. He took them shopping and bought them each their own glove and hat. He bought some Rawlings® glove oil and showed them how to break their gloves in. He did everything from running over the gloves with the car to putting them under the leg of the couch. I thought the whole ritual was a bit much, but I could see that they were all thoroughly enjoying the time spent with their father. He bought a bat and some balls and immediately started playing catch with them, preparing them to handle themselves on the field. He also took all four of his sons to the batting cages every chance he got. Ron Ron was already quite the baseball expert; able to hit 90 mph pitches by the time he was twelve. The boys would always come home from their trip to the cages bragging about how their big brother was able to hit the ball at 100 mph.

Ronald spared no expense when it came to buying things for his sons. On each of their birthdays he showered them with so many gifts, at times I thought he went a bit overboard. He may have been trying to make up for the years he was away. Each year for Christmas we had a theme for their presents. One year it was all things Ninja Turtles; turtle action figures, including their archenemies, Rhino man, Pizza face, and Genghis Frog. He bought them the turtle party van, turtle lunch pails, turtle weapons, shields, and masks. The next Christmas, it was fighting gear. We bought boxing gloves, hand wraps, headgear, mouth guards, pads, nun-chucks, and a heavy punching bag. They were always beside themselves on Christmas morning, and Ronald and I loved every moment of it.

～

A few months after he moved in with us, Ron Ron brought a young girl home and introduced her as his girlfriend. He was spending all of his time with her, and they appeared to be head over heels in love. Before long, our home had practically become her home. But because of our religious roots, Ronald and I could not condone premarital sex taking place under our roof. We made the mistake of insisting that they get married. Unfortunately, it was a brief and turbulent marriage; lasting for less than two years.

~

When we rented the house on Thirty-eighth Place, we hadn't considered just how deep in the "hood" we would be living until after we moved, and it was time to enroll the boys in school. Some friends from church told us about a private, Christian school they would be able to attend. The problem was that they only had openings for Daniel and Sir Darryl. We enrolled the two of them in L.A. Christian School, but Davion had to attend the local public school; James A. Foshay Junior High School. I was nervous about him having to be there every day, and it turned out that my nervousness was not unfounded.

Up until this time, Daniel was the son most known for fighting. But Davion had only been at the new school for a couple of weeks when he called me just before three o'clock, saying that he had gotten into a fight.

"Mom, can you come get me, please? I just got jumped!" I immediately felt my temperature rise, beginning at the top of my head, and spreading down into my chest, then radiating out into each of my limbs. "Jumped?!" I couldn't believe what I was hearing. I knew Davion to be one of the kindest, most loving kids ever. I was also aware that there was something about being the new kid that made school bullies feel like they needed to test him, but the fight was not fair. When the main instigator realized that Davion was not afraid of him and was ready and willing to stand up for himself, he called on two of his friends to help beat

Dave up. The largest of the three boys held Davion down while the other boys punched him.

Within minutes, I was speeding up to the school campus, at the gate where Davion told me to meet him. He was standing there alone, still fighting back tears in an attempt to minimize the damage. This was the first time someone had ever intentionally brought harm to one of my children, and I felt absolutely homicidal.

The kids were only allowed to leave through the gate where I met Dave, so we waited. I instructed him to point them out to me as soon as he saw them.

"There they are," he said, pointing to a man-sized kid and two smaller boys headed toward the gate. The rage I felt canceled out any fear I may have had under different circumstances. It didn't matter to me that the boy was nearly six feet tall. At that moment, he was a threat to my son, and I was there to countermand that threat.

"What's your name?" I said as I placed myself directly in his path.

"DeAndre," he answered with a puzzled look on his face.

"Let me tell you something DeAndre, you see that kid over there?" I said, pointing to Davion.

"Yeah," he answered. His words nearly got stuck in his throat when he realized who was standing in front of him.

"That's my son, and if you ever touch him again—if any of you ever put your hands on him again," I turned to confront the other boys Dave had pointed out to me.

"I won't just whip your ass, I will kill you!" I said, pointing my finger directly in his face. I continued my rant for a few minutes, speaking to each of the three culprits, convincing them that my threat was real.

"And I want you to go home and tell your mama what I said!" Just as those words came out of my mouth, one of the school officials came walking out of the gate.

"What's going on?" he asked.

"These boys jumped on my son earlier today, and I'm here to make sure nothing like that ever happens again!" Just as the young man opened his mouth to say something, I interrupted.

"And it's a good thing I am here—because I don't see nobody else handling this. Where were you when they were beatin' on my son?"

"Ma'am, I'm sorry about what happened, but I can't have you out here threatening to kill . . ." I interrupted again.

"I can't have nobody puttin' their hands on my son. And I'm not making idle threats. I'm telling you what's going to happen if these fools ever touch my son again!" I could hear chuckles from the crowd as they began to disburse, but the three boys stood there as if waiting to be dismissed. The young man asked if I wanted to come to the office and make a report, but I declined. I just wanted to take my baby home.

A few days later Kelvin, the main instigator, decided it wasn't over. He was embarrassed by the fact that Davion's mother had "punked" him in front of the other kids, and he felt the need to defend his honor. He squared off with Dave on the basketball court, expecting his boys to help him again. But I had made a believer out of DeAndre, and he left Kelvin to fight on his own. Just like before, the fight was not fair. Davion whipped Kelvin's ass and sent him crying with his tail between his legs. Of course, Davion had no more problems from that point on.

In between school and sports, I was still adamant about continuing the boys' musical education. By this time, they had developed their own little repertoire of favorites to sing, such as "The Reason Why I Sing" by Kirk Franklin and "Thank You" by Boyz II Men. These two songs were on the top of their list. People were always amazed at their ability to sing such tight harmony, but to them, it had become second nature.

N3D

On May 23, 1996, Ronald took the boys with him to pick up his check. His boss, E.J. Jackson was celebrating his birthday with a little barbecue at the office on West Boulevard. Eager to show off their musical talent, Ronald asked the boys to sing happy birthday. They started in unison, then broke into harmony when they got to the third line, and E.J. was blown away. He immediately picked up the phone and put in a call to Jheryl Busby, the man who spent many years as the president and CEO of Motown Records and was in the process of opening the R&B division of DreamWorks records. Within two hours Davion, Daniel, and Sir Darryl were in the studio recording their first demo. *Tell me what you want from me, am I just a wanna be? Wanna be your one and only love. And if you're liking what you see every time you look at me, tell me I'm your one and only love.* That little adolescent melody was enough to get the boys a record deal with DreamWorks. Only nine, ten, and eleven years of age, N3D was joining the ranks of hip-hop kiddy groups. Mr. Busby connected us with Donald Walton, an entertainment attorney, and within a few weeks, he was assisting us in negotiating their contract.

At first, I didn't know whether to be happy about the opportunity our kids faced or to be afraid of where this path would take them. I was aware of the cutthroat nature of the entertainment industry and the tragic end that many child celebrities faced. Even in the midst of my excitement, there was a part of me that wanted to protect my sons from potential tragedy. But there was another part of me that was thrilled with what was going on and hoped for their ultimate success.

"Please daddy can I have the keys to the car, promise you I won't go very far. I just wanna get away, see the world, take a little ride, just me and my girl." Up to this point, I had only written gospel songs, but this song flowed through my mind just as if God had placed it there. Ronald and I anticipated a conflict between school and career, so we decided to home-school the boys. The flexibility of our schedule would allow us to have them in the studio during some days and studying on others.

I knew enough about the music business to understand that the songwriters and producers held the greatest financial stake in the project, so I insisted that the boys be a part of the songwriting process. At the age of eighteen, I wrote my first song, *Perpetual Praise.* I should not have been surprised at how songwriting came naturally to my sons, but I was blown away by the ease at which they were able to create.

Mr. Busby brought in a young producer by the name of Gregg Pagani. At our first meeting with Gregg, he played several tracks for us. Once we all agreed on the best one, we began throwing around topic ideas. This style of writing was new to me. I had been accustomed to sitting down at the piano and writing the music, melody, and lyrics all at the same time. But this was the way of the industry, and my sons had no problem contributing significantly to the first song, "Already Have A Girl." Sir Darryl wasn't thrilled about the whole idea of being part of a group, but I noticed a light in his eyes during our songwriting sessions. He became more vocal than he had ever been, coming up with brilliant ideas and lyrics. As the youngest and most independent of his brothers, I didn't expect much from him, but it was during this time that I got my first glimpse of the brilliance and creativity of the artist, my little Sir.

Jheryl Busby was extremely hands-on with the boys, often inviting us to his beautiful home in Hancock Park to swim. He also arranged for them to work with Randy Gill, (Johnny Gill's brother) as a vocal coach. Over the next year, N3D received a $50,000 advance from the record label, had several photo-shoots, recorded four songs, and performed at a few local engagements to get their feet wet. But that was as far as they were able to go before Mr. Busby became ill. All work ceased because he was the one who had been personally handling the group. Weeks turned into months and, before we knew it, an entire year had gone by without a word from DreamWorks or Jheryl Busby. We finally had to accept the reality that this deal was going nowhere. I was both relieved *and* disappointed. But now, my sons could go on with normal life, which I truly believed was the best thing for them.

MR. BROOKS

Avery Brooks gained national recognition in a television series called *Spenser For Hire*, playing alongside Robert Urich in 1985. That led to a spin-off show of his own entitled *A Man Called Hawk*, the coolest brother on television at that time. Mr. Brooks is most known for his role as Captain Benjamin Sisko, the first Black captain on the *Star Trek: Deep Space Nine* television series. With his rich, distinct, and eloquent voice, he was often called on to narrate documentaries or as the voice for commercials. Avery has an intimidating persona and seems larger-than-life; but in reality, he is one of the most down-to-earth, kind, and thoughtful human beings one could ever have the pleasure of meeting. Ronald experienced that pleasure the day Mr. Brooks got in the back of his limousine.

The two of them immediately connected, and Mr. Brooks began requesting Ronald for all of his trips. Before long, Ronald had become his personal driver. He would come home every day with a new story about how and why he enjoyed working for Avery. Once, Ronald even brought him by our house and invited him in to meet the family. As he walked through the door, I wanted to jump up and down and scream *"Avery Brooks is IN MY HOUSE!,"* but I remained cool, not allowing my excitement to show. The boys didn't have a clue who they were meeting. They were their usual bubbly, polite, and respectful selves. Mr. Brooks was thoroughly impressed with Ronald's family, which endeared them to each other all the more.

Of course, Ronald insisted that the boys sing for Mr. Brooks before he left. By this time, they had mastered their repertoire, and broke out in their favorite *Boys-2-Men* song:

> *"I was young (BOP), and didn't have nowhere to run, I needed to WAKE-UP, and see what's in front of me, nah nah nah! There has to be a better way, sing it again a better way, to show I'm grateful, YEAH-OOP . . ."*

We always got the same reaction when people heard the boys sing this song. Mr. Brooks was blown away. "I've got to find a way to get them on the show," he said in his authoritative, matter-of-fact tone, his voice bellowing through the room like the roar of Mufasa. He was referring to *Star Trek: Deep Space Nine.* That moment was truly surreal. Several weeks went by before we heard anything more about the boys appearing on the show. But during that time Ronald continued to drive Mr. Brooks daily. After a few weeks, it occurred to Ronald that he was doing all the driving, but E.J. was getting all the money. Since he had become Avery Brooks' personal driver, it seemed more practical for Ronald to get his own town car, and to cut out the middleman. Ronald went into business for himself and purchased a black, 1996 Cadillac Fleetwood Brougham.

Mr. Brooks took time out of his busy schedule to treat our family to a trip to Magic Mountain. And he didn't just give us the money to go; he went with us. Ronald and I, Davion, Daniel, and Darryl spent the day with Avery Brooks and his three children, Cabral, Asante, and Ayana. We already thought very highly of him, but this gesture was above and beyond anything we would ever have anticipated from a man of his stature. It showed us just how special he was. But the kindness didn't stop there. One day, he noticed that Ronald wasn't his usual, jovial self.

"Mr. Farris, is everything alright? How's the family?" He was genuinely concerned.

"Everything's fine. I just miss my wife. She's on a three-week tour in Europe. And when she comes home she has to turn right around and go to Australia." Ronald explained. Without hesitation, Mr. Brooks uttered three simple words, "You should go." He pulled out his cell phone, and within fifteen minutes, he had purchased a round-trip ticket to Sydney, Australia so Ron could visit me. Rena stayed at the house and kept the boys while Ronald and I enjoyed our time together in Sydney. I was singing background for a young artist named Joshua Kadison, and we performed practically every night on the tour. The manager arranged for us to have one day off in Sydney, and I was able to spend it on a boat with my husband, taking pictures in front of one of the most famous and distinctive structures in the world: the Sydney Opera House.

Not long after we returned home, Mr. Brooks told us that he would be directing a special episode of the show entitled *Far Beyond the Stars*, a whimsical, sci-fi story of a twisted, time-travel hallucination. It was set in the 1950s and, as director, Avery was able to have the boys appear in one of the scenes as a street singing, doo-wop group. They were only on camera for about thirty seconds, but that was the most exciting thirty seconds of their lives. Ronald and I watched in amazement as our sons worked on the set of *Star Trek* with Captain Sisko, receiving VIP treatment the entire day. It was an unforgettable experience. Ronald continued driving Mr. Brooks until they taped the last episode in June of 1999. We were sad to see that season come to an end, but the impression he made on our lives remains to this day.

Mr. Brooks was not the only celebrity that Ronald brought to our home to meet his family. Marques Houston, Jerome Jones and Don Santos, better known as the R&B group, *Immature*, were scheduled to be presenters at the 1996 Grammy awards but needed to stop and change into their tuxedos. They wanted to avoid the rush, and we only lived a few miles away from the venue, so Ronald conveniently offered to bring them to our house. They were a few years older than our sons and were living the life that N3D dreamed of. Ronald knew that the boys would be thrilled to meet them. He made sure they took plenty of pictures. It was a day our sons would never forget.

DAVION

CHAPTER SIX
YOUNG MEN

In 1998, we had to say goodbye to Ronald's grandmother, Essie Burkley. She held the position of the rock and matriarch of the Burkley family for decades; it felt like the end of an era. Essie worked for many years as a janitor in the L.A. Unified School District, saved her money, and bought several properties. Ronald's mother, Mattie, had been plagued by addiction and incarceration for many years, but Grandma Essie stepped in and took care of all her grandchildren, and even her great-grandson, Ron Ron.

After she passed, we purchased the home in which she had raised Ronald and his siblings. Park Circle was now home to the Farris family, and the boys were ecstatic. They were twelve, thirteen, and fourteen years old and the next few years would prove to be some of the best years of our lives. I was still working for the same church and our entire family attended faithfully every Sunday. Ron Ron and his rap group, KPS was loved by the entire congregation—that is until one of the church mothers smelled marijuana on them and complained to the pastor. They were no longer allowed to minister, and we were all heartbroken. Ron Ron was so devastated that he left the church, never to return, which engraved a permanent scar on my soul.

THE LOS ANGELES MISSION

The Los Angeles Mission, located downtown in the heart of skid row is a place where the homeless can come in daily, receive a hot meal, and a warm place to sleep at night. The only requirement is that they attend the afternoon chapel service first. They also provide a twelve-month, live-in rehabilitation program.

Ronald's days as a limousine driver came to an end when he was offered a position as Chaplain at the Mission. This was perfect for him because he was able to guide a group of men down the same path to sobriety that he had successfully navigated. Ronald would often ask the boys and me to sing at the afternoon chapel services. We also performed at their annual Thanksgiving and Christmas extravaganzas. Each year, they would cordon off entire city blocks, set up stages, prepare holiday meals and give gifts to thousands in need. Ronald was in his element working with the men at the mission. It was a source of pride for him.

Ronald's job at the Mission enabled us to do much more as a family than we had ever been able to do before. We purchased timeshare property and took the boys on vacation as often as we could. Big Bear, Lake Tahoe, San Diego, Puerto Escondido, and Rosarito Beach were some of our favorite spots. The life that we were now living felt like an extension of many of my childhood experiences. Each time we took our sons on vacation, I was reminded of trips to Val Verde, Big Bear, or Disneyland with my parents. It was extremely gratifying for us to be able to restore the dream that was lost when my mom and dad divorced. That dream not only included our children but also one or more of their friends. Emmanuel, Moses, Tony, or Evan would sometimes accompany us on these trips.

~

Amid our family excursions and blossoming ministry, my career continued to flourish. Besides singing background for major artists, one of my main sources of income was singing demos for producers and songwriters, and I was able to work with some of the best in the business. Gerry Goffin was among those who hired me to bring his music to life. Gerry, along with his wife, Carole King, was responsible for penning such hits as "Will You Love Me Tomorrow," "My Imagination," and the Aretha Franklin mega-hit, "Natural Woman." It was an honor for me to have the opportunity to work with such a legend. Despite his status, he seemed to be equally as thrilled to work with me. He initially hired me to sing his demos to try and sell them to other artists, but after hearing my voice on his music, he decided to pitch the songs to record companies.

Gerry decided that together we would become the next Clive Davis and Whitney Houston. When he told me what he had in mind, of course, I was all for it. He set up several meetings with executives from different labels and they all seemed to be interested. I thought this would be my big break, but after several months passed and no real offers were on the table, I slowly began to lose hope. I was thankful to have my job at the church, and as time went on, I found more satisfaction in singing praises to God each Sunday than I ever imagined I would.

Upon the first encounter with my church, Bible Enrichment, in 1989, I knew right away that there was something special about it. Even after a lifetime of church attendance, I had never heard that kind of teaching. God had prepared me for the position of worship leader under Pastor Bam's ministry, and it was a special connection. It took me a while to learn that becoming a celebrated secular artist was not a part of my destiny. After a few years of leading worship, it became much more than a job to me, it became my passion. My brother, Anthony, joined the church shortly after I began working there and was a part of the praise team. The two of us wrote many of the songs that we sang for praise and worship on Sunday morning. Songs like "All Day," "You Don't Have To Tell Me Twice," "Praise & Worship," "In the Presence of the Lord," "So Nice," and many others became a regular part of our Sunday morning worship experience. One of our most memorable praise and worship songs happened to be the very first song I wrote at the age of eighteen, "Perpetual Praise."

"Perpetual praise and continual prayer take the joy of the Lord with you everywhere. Perpetual prayer and continual praise, acknowledge Him in all of your ways!" It appeared that everyone who attended the church was impacted by our music. One song, in particular, seemed to have the greatest effect on all who heard it, "My Help." This song was special because of all the songs I'd ever written, this is the only one that came to me in a dream. God literally gave me this song while I was sleeping. Although I am the one who got up in the morning, went to the piano, and wrote it down, I cannot fully take credit for writing it because it was almost as if it was being dictated to me. The anointing on our worship, and especially on this song impacted everyone who experienced the service, including Lorena Munson, a record executive, and friend of Pastor Bam. She was so moved by the power of the music at Bible Enrichment that she offered us a record deal.

We had to come up with a name for the group, so we had a meeting with the leaders in the music department. *Bible Enrichment Choir* felt a bit corny, so we threw around several ideas until we finally came up with the name *Bam Crawford's Purpose*, since everything had come together under her ministry.

"My Help" was a huge hit. The Brooklyn Tabernacle Choir, as well as popular gospel artists Ron & CeCe Winans and Donnie McClurkin recorded the song, which earned it international acclaim.

TASHA SMITH

One Sunday after church, a young lady who had recently become a member came to me and introduced herself. She told me how much my music ministry had blessed her. I responded by telling her that she was as much a blessing to me as I had been to her. Because of her bubbly personality and passionate worship, she stood out in the congregation. Seeing people engaged in worship like her always made me feel like I was doing a good job as worship leader. She was a beautiful girl; tall and slender with big bushy hair. She had a bright, infectious smile and captivating energy. Her name was Tasha Smith.

"We should get together sometimes," she said. That was a phrase I heard often, but in many cases, I was hesitant to accept the invitation for one reason or another. This time, however, was different. I didn't sense anything behind her words but sincerity. She was someone I wanted to get to know. Within a few weeks, Tasha and I met for lunch and it was wonderful. It was refreshing to meet someone with whom I enjoyed spending time. Being a wife, mother and minister was beautiful, but it always came with its demands. Hanging out with Tasha was pure and simple fun.

I invited my new friend to the house to meet my family and have dinner. As soon as she met the boys, she was smitten.

"Oh my God, they are soooooo adorable! These boys should be on TV!" She said. They had the same type of effect on Tasha that they'd had on E.J. Jackson and Avery Brooks. She immediately made a phone call and connected them with her agent. We set up another photoshoot so the boys could have individual headshots. The only pictures they had taken up to that point were group shots. Once the photos were done, the agent began sending them out on auditions. Tasha coached them in acting and the audition process. She was unable, however, to prepare them for the disappointment of being turned down most of the time. In entertainment, it's common to book only a very small percentage of the shows for which you audition. Sometimes, you don't book anything at all. This was the case with the boys. They went out on dozens of auditions but seemed to be unable to get a call back. After several months, Davion and Sir Darryl gave up on acting. But something inside Daniel kept him from giving up, and it eventually paid off.

～

Daniel's hair was very long and he either wore it in a big Afro, or I would occasionally braid it in cornrows for him. When he wore his braids, he looked more like a thug than the intellectual, gifted musician that he was. It didn't matter to him that he was always being cast as a thug, as long as he was being cast. Within a month after his brothers gave up, Daniel landed a small role on a television series called *Boston Public*. Not long after that, he was booked for another part on a television drama entitled, *Judging Amy*. He also booked a small role in a movie entitled, *Our America*. He was almost chosen for the lead role but was unable to work the amount of hours required for the lead because he was too young.

Daniel worked on a few more episodes of *Boston Public* before he landed the most unforgettable of any of his roles. Daniel played the part of a murderous gang member on the television series, *The District*. He was the center of a defining scene in which he rode on his small BMX-type bike through downtown Los Angeles. He held the handlebars with his left hand and a Glock pistol down by his right side. After riding a few blocks, he pulled the gun up from his side and began shooting. People scattered in all directions, but he was still able to hit his intended target. He then jumped off his bike allowing it to fall to the ground, took a few steps, and fired one last shot, point-blank into his victim, finishing the job.

The last part of the scene was shot with the cameraman lying on the ground and Daniel standing over him, so we saw it from the perspective of the victim. A chill went to my core as I watched because of the uncanny realism of the moment. It was as if I was watching my fifteen-year-old son commit murder. Even though he didn't have any lines, he played the role with such emotional accuracy that every move he made, every expression on his face helped to tell the story. There was clearly a part of my sons' experience that he was able to draw from.

The life of a young Black man in Inglewood was filled with unique challenges. Neighborhoods were separated by gang lines of red or blue, and we happened to live in a red zone. This meant that whether we liked it or not, we were governed by certain unwritten rules that, if ignored, could cost a young man his life. Ron Ron had taught his little brothers those rules and constantly schooled them on how to carry themselves. His teaching, however, was not able to shield them from some inevitable confrontations by rival gangs.

One day after school, Daniel and his brothers came walking into the house in a fit of anger and frustration because grown men had just banged on them, meaning; challenged them in a threatening manner. As soon as they told me what happened, I headed for the door to go and find the culprit.

"Mom! Where are you going?" they asked, practically in unison.

"I'm going to find these fools so I can set 'em straight!" The mother-bear in me didn't realize that it was no longer my job to protect my cubs.

"NOOO Mom, you can't do that!" They nearly had to physically restrain me, but I eventually listened to what they were saying and decided to leave it alone.

I was baffled by the mindset of a gang-banger. I will never understand the claiming of territory that you don't own and making enemies out of your own people. It vexed my soul that my sons were forced to learn the boundaries on the invisible gang map, each gang's colors, dances, and gang hand signs. At first, I just saw them as terrorists, but in time I learned that many of them were friends, neighbors, or classmates who, like my boys, had fathers who were serving long sentences for drug-related crimes. My sons went to school with the gang members, laughed with them, balled with them in the park, and grew up with them. Daniel tells the story of one of their most frightening encounters with some gang members:

"It was a familiar face that saved our lives. We were walking down Kelso Street crossing Flower after school, on our way back from the Inglewood YMCA when a car sped down the street so fast that we all watched in amazement. We thought they would do donuts and peel out like the usual street shows we'd witnessed. However, just as the car passed us, they hit a U-turn, burning rubber the entire way, sending smoke into the air from the rear tires. The car then stopped and three brown teenagers not far from our own age climbed halfway out of the window and sat just on the sill with their legs still inside the car. We just stood there and looked, still not aware that this entire display was for us. Then suddenly, almost in unison, all of the youngsters started banging their gangs, shouting the name of their neighborhood while twisting their fingers up to visually represent their hood.

They "dissed" the rival gang native to the neighborhood where we happened to be walking, obviously assuming that we were members of that gang. At that moment everything slowed down. I looked closely at each figure. One had his hand near his lap and was holding a dark pistol about 9 inches long. The others didn't have their other hand out at all, which left me to assume that each of them was armed. Then I looked at the face of the third and realized that he went to our school. I had seen him every day and even shared a class with him. He never said much but always spoke when he passed. This time, when I noticed his face, I just put my hands up and stood there and shook my head as if to say, 'it's not us.' I caught eyes with my associate from school and watched as he connected with the fear that I was experiencing at the moment. Right then, he nearly panicked. He began reaching for the other guys hanging out of the car shouting, 'it's not them! It's not them!' Almost immediately they climbed back nto the car and the driver sped off as one of them shouted the name of his gang one last time as if disappointed from a failed encounter.

Not every encounter was like this, but having this experience changed how we viewed even the most subtle exchange with other youngsters. We were inherently conflicted, aware of our mortality far too early, traumatized by people who looked like us and walked our same path."

Many years passed before my sons told me about that episode. They knew I wouldn't have been able to handle it. I'm so grateful that it played out the way it did. The thought of losing my babies to gang violence is unimaginable. I was often accused of being overly protective of my boys, but I was never concerned with what other people thought. Even Ronald accused me of being too much of a mother hen.

"Let those boys be boys," he would always say. He wanted them to catch the bus to school, but I hated the idea and often drove them. As soon as Daniel turned sixteen, we allowed him to buy a car with the money that he'd earned from acting. He bought a brand new, silver Honda Civic hatchback. I felt better knowing that my sons no longer needed to rely on public transportation.

Daniel had proven that he could be trusted with the privilege of owning a car. He had always been a unique kid. Even at the age of seven, he began to establish his independence. At night he would pick his clothes for school the next day. He would even iron them and lay them out neatly. He also meticulously prepared his lunch at night and made sure he was ready to face whatever challenge might come his way the following day. Daniel was the only one of his brothers that asked if he could wash the dishes. Actually, he is the only person I've ever known who *wanted* to clean the kitchen at age seven.

Before his first day in high school, Daniel had made up his mind that he would receive straight A's in all of his classes. He came to this conclusion at his middle school graduation when he saw who had been awarded the title of valedictorian.

"I know I'm smarter than her!" He declared. He hated the idea that his grades weren't a true reflection of his level of intelligence. So, he made the determination never to let that happen again, and he was able to accomplish this goal until the second semester of his sophomore year. On the day that the progress reports were sent home, Daniel stormed in the front door. It was clear that he was livid. He was fuming with anger because he received a C in one of his classes. Out of all the classes to get a low grade in, he'd gotten a C in music.

I knew immediately that there had been some kind of mistake. There was no way he deserved a C in anything, especially music, the very thing that I had been teaching him his entire life. Daniel had managed to get an A in every other class, in every semester. Whether it was honors English or algebra II, Daniel got an A. He always took the time to establish a rapport with his teachers, and all of them loved having a student like Daniel in their class—all except the music teacher. Daniel was a bit too much of a challenge for him. As his mother, I began to learn how to deal with his demanding nature when he was only eight months old and refused to stay in the playpen. I'd learned to respect his brilliant young mind. I allowed all of my sons the space to determine who they wanted to be, and how they wanted to be. But the music teacher hadn't had the privilege of years of experience dealing with the genius that was Daniel Anthony Farris.

"I got a C in music," he said, fighting back tears. He was so angry he could hardly contain himself. As soon as I heard what he said, it was as if he transferred his anger to me.

"WHAT?" I really couldn't believe what I was hearing. It didn't make sense.

"WHY?," I asked, not really caring what the answer was. I had already concluded that the teacher had made a grave error, one that I was certain he would correct after I spoke to him.

Still fuming, Daniel explained the incident that was supposedly at the root of the problem.

"We were on the bus, getting ready to go to a Martin Luther King Day parade and I was wearing a wave cap so my braids would look fresh when we got there. I wasn't planning to wear it all day. Mr. Dickerson yelled at me and told me to take that ghetto thing off my head. I took it off, then he snatched it from me, and he gave it to his wife. When he got off and went to the other bus, I asked her to give it back to me. I wasn't going to put it back on, I just didn't feel like it was right for him to take my stuff from me and keep it. She said okay and told me not to put it back on. I put it in my backpack and thought everything was cool. But when he got back on the bus and found out that I asked her for it, he kicked me off the bus. My participation in the parade was half of my final grade."

I knew immediately that there was much more to it than the bus incident. Mr. Dickerson was either intimidated, threatened or just plain envious of Daniel's talent and his brilliant mind. He found a weird sense of satisfaction in exercising power over him. Well, I was one of those parents who was not about to allow this man to ruin my son's perfect record because of his ego.

"Don't worry 'bout nothing baby! We're going up there first thing in the morning and I promise you, your grade will be an A when I'm done!" Daniel breathed a sigh of relief. He was confident that I would be able to do exactly what I said. The next morning, Ronald decided that he would go in to work late so he could be with me when we confronted Daniel's teacher. He wasn't as concerned about me as he was the teacher. Ronald had come to know a side of me as a mother that he had never seen in his young bride. I was always calm, and almost passive at times until someone threatened one of my sons. He knew that what I had to say to Mr. Dickerson wasn't going to be nice, so he came along as a buffer.

The next morning, we walked straight into the principal's office and told her secretary that we needed to speak with her immediately. Ronald kept his hand on my shoulder, massaging it the entire time.

"What can I do for you, Mr. and Mrs. Farris?" Ms. Tate, the principal, was very cordial. She was quite fond of Daniel, and almost as proud of him as we were. I knew better than to jump down her throat, so I kept my anger at bay.

"Well, Ms. Tate" I began to explain, "We received Daniel's progress report yesterday and it had a C on it."

"A 'C'?" She was dumbfounded. "In which class?" she asked.

"In his music class," I responded.

"Oh no! That has to be a mistake." The more she spoke, the more I realized that it wasn't going to be a problem at all. She understood the importance of the student's record when it came to applying for college. She called her secretary in and instructed her to have Mr. Dickerson come to the office right away, which instantly put my mind at ease. She spent the next ten minutes singing Daniel's praises while we waited for his teacher to arrive. I was tickled, realizing that my work was already done. However, I was still anxiously awaiting Mr. Dickerson's arrival so I could let him have it.

As soon as he walked in the door, she began questioning him.

"So what happened that made you give Daniel Farris a C? You know he's received nothing but A's since he's been here. That C would completely ruin his perfect record."

"Well, you know we don't give out grades based on a student's past performance, but on how well they perform in our class," he said, trying to justify what he had done. It was now my turn to respond.

"Here's the problem with that Mr., what's your name?"

"Dickerson," he answered.

"Mr. Dickerson, the problem with that grade is that I know my son. And there's no way that his performance in your class deserves a C. Daniel is NOT a C student! Now, he told me about the situation on the bus, and that had absolutely nothing to do with how he should have been graded." Ronald was still rubbing my shoulder in an effort to limit the crescendo that was taking place in my tone.

"I understand what you're saying Mrs. Farris, but . . ." I interrupted him.

"I didn't come down here to debate with you about whether or not Daniel deserves a C, I came to tell you that you are going to change that grade to an A. It's not your job to grade students based on your ego! That was a childish thing for you to do—to kick him off the bus for asking for what belonged to him, and then blame HIM for not participating in the event that YOU prevented him from going to!"

"Calm down baby." Ronald felt the heat rising from my shoulder. So I took a deep breath. Before I could begin another sentence, Ms. Tate jumped in.

"What's this about the situation on the bus?" she said, directing her words to Mr. Dickerson.

"Last week, we were leaving for the MLK parade when Mr. Farris got on the bus wearing that ghetto do-rag . . ." before he could say another word, I interrupted again.

"He wasn't planning on wearing it all day. He just wanted his braids to look fresh when he got off the bus. But YOU didn't take the time to find that out. You just spoke to him and treated him like he was a dumb kid, which you are well aware that he's NOT. And because you didn't like his response, you chose to exercise your power over him, and then punish him, instead of treating him with the same respect that you feel like you deserve. I'm his mother, and I don't even treat him the way you did! And I refuse to allow you and your ego to ruin my son's perfect record!"

The room was quiet for a beat, and then Ms. Tate spoke again.

"I'm afraid I'm going to have to agree with Mrs. Farris on this one Mr. Dickerson. What can we do?"

After a few moments of discussion, they agreed to allow Daniel to do a musical performance as a way to make up his final. He chose Fantasie Impromptu by Chopin. Mr. Dickerson, Ms. Tate, Ronald, and I stood around the upright piano in the band room while Daniel flawlessly performed the piece with passion. His left hand pounded the lower register, releasing the frustration of the undeserved blemish with every note. His right hand graced the upper notes with precision, completely dispelling any inkling of doubt in his musical abilities, work ethic, or discipline. When the song ended, no one had any questions about what the grade would be. He made his statement, and we achieved our mission that day.

Ronald and I didn't have many disagreements when it came to raising our sons. But one thing we were never able to agree on was when, where, and how they would learn to drive. I learned very early and was able to handle myself behind the wheel at age thirteen. So by the time I was old enough to get my driver's license, I'd had plenty of experience. I wanted to begin teaching my sons when they were in their early teens, but Ronald believed that we should wait until they could get their permit, and then leave the training up to the driver's education teachers. We argued over the issue several times until I decided simply to take matters into my own hands. The thought of my sons driving around on the streets of Los Angeles was scary enough. I was determined to make sure they had plenty of experience behind the wheel by the time they turned sixteen.

I thought I would be able to discreetly keep it from Ronald, but that was easier said than done. The very first time I took Davion driving around the neighborhood, he ran up on a curb, barely missing some pedestrians, and put a hefty, little dent in the front fender. Of course, I had to tell Ronald the truth about how it happened. He was upset with me for going against his wishes, but he realized how determined I was and agreed that we would begin teaching the boys to drive, but only in the parking lot of the Great Western Forum where there was practically nothing to run into. Both Ronald and I continued teaching them until I had some degree of confidence in their driving ability.

We never had any real disciplinary problems out of our sons. I attribute that to two things; first of all, I was a hands-on mother. When they were small, I was extremely attentive. I nurtured and developed a respectful and loving relationship with all of my boys, but I did it with a firm hand. As toddlers, I didn't let them get away with unruly behavior.

I established boundaries early, and at times I had to physically enforce those boundaries. But I didn't have to do it often and, whenever I did, I was careful not to cross the line from discipline to abuse. After their father came home, I didn't have to do it at all.

Ronald was as attentive as I was, sometimes even more. We always kept them involved in some type of activity. When they weren't playing little league baseball, they were taking karate lessons. When they weren't doing vocal exercises, they were practicing the piano. I did my best to give the boys all that I had, teach them all I knew, and love them with all my heart. Ronald's motivation to be a good father to his sons came largely from the void left by his father. He has only one memory of his dad taking him to a Dodger game when he was twelve, but that's it. The man who was supposed to be his father basically deserted him, leaving him with the desire to be the father that he never had, and he did just that.

Once they became teenagers, there was only one incident in which I had to deal with direct rebellion and disrespect. One day, Davion asked if he could go hang out with his friends. I said no, but he decided to go anyway. I could not believe that he so blatantly disregarded my words. I had never given my sons any reason to disrespect me. I was always fair, loving, patient, and generous toward them. They were the light of my life, and I loved them unconditionally. But when Dave decided that he would simply ignore me and do what he wanted, it struck a nerve that I didn't realize I had. Several thoughts went through my mind. I imagined myself jumping on him and beating him down, but he was far too big for that. Then I imagined putting him out of my house and telling him that he was on his own, but he was only fifteen.

Davion stayed away for a few hours, but when he returned I told him that the two of us were going out to dinner so we could talk. He looked puzzled. He knew I was angry and couldn't possibly imagine what I had in mind. His brothers were equally as puzzled as he was. They knew what he had done and couldn't figure out why I was taking him out to dinner instead of them.

We went to Houston's Restaurant in Redondo Beach. I needed his undivided attention, and I also needed a pleasant atmosphere to help get my point across. My anger made me realize that my unconditional love for my sons did have certain conditions.

"Dave, you know you were wrong, don't you?" I said calmly.

"Yes, I know. I'm sorry mom." I could tell that he was genuinely remorseful for his actions, and all the more, now that I was treating him so kindly.

"I need you to understand something. As your mother, no one in this world loves you more than I do, no one has your back like I do. Whenever you need something, I am always willing to do whatever it takes to see to it that you have it. If you had no place to go, you'd always have a home with me. I would go hungry so you could eat. I would literally die for you Davion." I could see that he was fighting to hold back tears.

"I've always been the type of woman that loves intensely. But when I feel betrayed, it's as if I have a switch inside me that immediately turns off that love. I always believed that only applied to my relationships with men, and I never imagined that switch could be turned off by one of my children. But what you did today made me realize that it could. I was so angry, so hurt, so disappointed in you that I could feel myself

almost wanting to cut you off! I didn't deserve that from you Davion."
At this point, he was no longer holding back his tears. I continued.

"I love you Davion, more than you could possibly even understand.
But if you ever disrespect me like that again, just know that you may
lose the greatest love in your life. And I don't think you wanna do that,
do you?"

"No." He was too choked up to say more, so we sat quietly and ate
our food. After a little time passed, he said again.

"I'm sorry mom. I'll never do that again." I could tell he meant what
he said.

~

Time really does fly. It seemed as if I was just making his lunch and
putting pencils and crayons in his backpack for the first day of
kindergarten. Now, Davion was graduating from high school. The
ceremony was held at the Great Western Forum, and it was unforgettable.
It began with the processional to *Pomp and Circumstance*. We heard
from the principal, the valedictorian, and the guest speaker. We then
watched the celebration of one family after another as their student's
name was called. It was a very large graduating class, so this took a
while. Once every student had walked across the stage and made it
back to their seats, the intro to a different song began. Starting from
the very last row, Davion walked slowly down the center aisle singing
Never can say goodbye, no no no no I, never can say goodbye. It was only a
high school graduation but, once again, I was as proud as if he were
performing at Carnegie Hall.

Music had always been Davion's first love. Despite being intellectually gifted, he didn't share Daniel's passion for academics. After graduation, he wanted to devote all of his time to the pursuit of his career, but his father laid out certain ground rules that he was required to follow if he was going to continue living with us.

"If you're not going to go to college, you have to get a job," Ronald insisted.

After Davion's graduation, Daniel was reigning as the student body president at Inglewood High School. Sir was in the eleventh grade, and he was one of the star players of the junior varsity basketball team. Daniel shares a memory of watching his brother play.

"We didn't grow up playing basketball as our primary sport, so I had no idea that once Sir started taking it seriously, he would become so good, so fast. One day I decided to hang out in the gym after school. JV was playing and my brother was on the court. My experience with basketball was such that I rarely got in the game and, when I did, nothing significant happened because I wasn't a baller. But when I went in to watch the game, he was playing defense on the other team's point guard.

During the seven minutes that I was there, Sir Darryl stole the ball, dunked on the dude that he stole the ball from, got right back on defense, and was looking at the guy like he hated him. He played with such passion. I was both proud and surprised, looking at my brother like, Who is this dude?"

Ronald's favorite memory of Sir Darryl on the basketball court took place when Inglewood played against high school powerhouse, Mater Dei. This was a playoff game, which determined who would go to the state championship. Sir Darryl entered the game late in the fourth quarter, mainly because he was a lock-down defender. With thirty seconds left in the game, Inglewood had the ball and the clock was winding down. Sir was posted up in a corner and Mater Dei's defense wasn't guarding him because they didn't expect him to shoot. With four seconds left on the shot clock, the point guard passed it to Sir. He took a step back, using what seemed like three of the four seconds he had left, elevated and put up a beautiful, eighteen-foot, three-point shot. It swished through the center of the hoop without even touching the rim. The Inglewood side of the gym went crazy. Sir's jumper gave them a six-point lead, sealing the win for Inglewood. During this season, his relationship with basketball was a bit more of a priority to him than music.

KELLY-ANN BOOTHE

Although Sir Darryl was able to ride with Daniel to school every day, he wanted a car of his own so he wouldn't be so dependent on his brother. We had assured the boys that if they kept their grades up we would allow them to have their own car when they got their license. Sir Darryl's grades were excellent, so we started shopping for a car. He came across a maroon, 1988 Honda Civic for sale in the gas station near his school. They were asking $1,500, but we offered them $1,100, and our offer was accepted. He had only been driving his car for a few days when I received a phone call.

"Mom, don't worry, I'm okay—but I had an accident." Even though I knew he was okay, my heart still dropped down into the pit of my stomach.

"Where are you?" I asked, "I'm on the 405 northbound, just past Manchester, and I need you to come right away." I immediately grabbed my keys and headed out the door.

"Was it your fault?" I asked from my cell phone, as I got in my car.

"Yeah, I rear-ended her. But it's not that bad. Her car is barely scratched."

We didn't live that far from the 405 freeway so I was pulling up behind him within ten minutes. Just as he said, the damage to the woman's car was minimal. I pulled the camera out and began filming. We exchanged information and she was on her way. As soon as the woman left, I noticed the woman that was in the car with Sir. She was dressed in a skirt and high heels—a beautiful, shapely young lady with long, thick hair.

"Mom, this is Kelly" I reached out to shake her hand, as I wondered what this grown woman was doing with my sixteen-year-old son.

"It's a pleasure to meet you, Mrs. Farris," she said with a smile, looking directly into my eyes. As I looked back at her, I realized that she wasn't the grown woman I thought she was. She was just dressed like one. Sir Darryl describes that night in his own words.

"That was the first time I had a girl in my car, and it was my first date with Kelly Ann Boothe. She was so beautiful, and I was excited that she agreed to go out with me. When I picked her up, she made it clear that nothing was going down that night. 'I don't know what you're expecting, but I'm just going out with you, and then you're taking me home.' I respected her for setting boundaries. We were on our way to Universal City Walk, and I kept looking over at her, admiring her beauty. She looked back and smiled. Again, I looked at her and she looked at me. I looked at her, she looked at me—I looked at her and

BAM! I ran into the car in front of me. The damage to my car was much more severe than the one I hit. But worse than that, I was embarrassed. It was clearly not that big a deal to Kelly, because she let me kiss her at the end of the date."

We had Sir's car towed to the mechanic's shop around the corner from the house. He asked if he could use my car, but I offered to drop them off and pick them up instead. Once the date was over and we dropped Kelly off at home, I knew by the smile on Sir Darryl's face that we would be seeing a lot more of Ms. Boothe.

Sir Darryl and Kelly had been dating for nearly a year when her mother died. They were originally from Jamaica and she and her sister had no other family in the states. They were left motherless and homeless. Kelly's sister had friends that she was able to live with, and Kelly moved in with us. Since I never had a daughter of my own, her presence in our household was truly a gift. Another extraordinary gift was soon to be bestowed on my three teenage musicians.

RON RON

KELLY-ANN

CHAPTER SEVEN

ADULTING

My older brother, Andrew Gouché, is known for being one of the pioneers of playing bass in the Gospel music world. Many consider him the G.O.A.T. He began in the late seventies playing for James Cleveland, Walter Hawkins, Andre Crouch, and the Winans. His career has spanned decades, with such credits as Chaka Kahn, Anita Baker, Gladys Knight, Prince, and numerous others. Andrew is also known for giving many successful young musicians their start in the music business by introducing them to the right people or hiring them for gigs. Although the deal with DreamWorks didn't work out, our sons never gave up on their dream of having a career in music.

When the boys were around thirteen, fourteen, and fifteen, Andrew was updating his studio and decided to hand his current equipment over to his nephews, enabling them to take the next step toward bringing their musical dreams to reality. He gave them a set of JBL speakers, a keyboard, Tascam cd burner, Alesis Nano Synth and Nano Bass sound modules, Planet Phatt sound module, a desktop computer with Cubase production software, a microphone, an MPC 2000 drum machine, a disc full of sounds, a desk with cables to hook everything up and a studio rack to mount all of their hardware. They convinced their father and me to allow them to convert the garage into a studio. With the advance money left over from DreamWorks, they purchased a "how-to" book on carpentry from Home Depot, and all the material they needed to design and build a recording studio. We were amazed at what they were able to accomplish.

They hired an electrician to help with the wiring and lighting, installed insulation, hardwood flooring, soundproof walls, and a vocal booth. They even built a desk for the mixing board, computer, and speakers. They decided to name the studio *Woodworks*, which eventually became the name of their production team. Woodworks consisted of Sir Darryl, Davion, Daniel, his best friend Emmanual, and their cousin Tiffany Gouché, my brother Anthony's oldest daughter. Tiffany's voice is as smooth as melted butter, and her overall musical gift is as prolific as her cousins.

Each of our sons had their own set of friends, and our home was like a second home to all of them. Sir Darryl was still good friends with Tony, LaRenee's nephew. Daniel connected with a bubbly young man named Emmanuel, and a fearless, rugged young man named Evan. Davion's crew consisted of Moses, Mike, and Clifford, who they referred to as "Bliff." All these young men had become an extension of our family and were often included on special occasions like trips to Knott's Berry Farm, Magic Mountain or family vacations.

Each of our boys had grown into mature, self-sufficient young men, with their own individual M.O. Sir preferred playing basketball, while

Davion and Daniel were either hanging with their friends, playing video games, or busy in the studio making music.

TIA & DAYLIN

After his graduation Davion got a job as a bank teller and made music when he wasn't working at the bank. He had been the first of the three younger boys to have a girlfriend. At the tender young age of ten, he declared his love for a girl he'd met in school by the name of Gladys Jackson. He told his father and me that he couldn't wait until he turned eighteen so he could get married, and we soon found out how serious he was. One evening after work, he came home with a young lady we had never met, with her newborn baby.

"Mom, Dad, this is Tia." He said with a giant smile on his face. "And this is Daylin," he said, pointing to the baby. I asked if I could hold him. As she handed the little guy to me, I was immediately overwhelmed with emotion.

"Why do I love this baby?" I had held plenty of babies before, but there was definitely something different about this one. I felt a connection to this little boy—as if he were my own grandchild. I wasn't quite sure what was going on. Was Davion the father? And if he *was*, why did he wait until the child was born to tell us?

"Can we go in the room and talk?" Davion wanted to offer some clarity, but not in front of everyone else. Still holding on to little Daylin, I got up from my seat, and Davion, Ronald, and I walked into our bedroom.

"I want to marry Tia," he said. Davion was only nineteen years old, and I immediately thought of the ten-year-old Dave who said that he couldn't wait until he was 18 so he could get married. I was at a loss for words, but Ronald wasn't.

"First of all, is this your son?" Ronald's tone was one of irritation. "Why are you just now telling us about him?"

"I don't know, dad, I wasn't ready before."

"And you're not ready to get married either! Where would you guys live? Do you make enough money at the bank to take care of a family?"

"I was thinking we could live here until we saved enough money to get our own apartment." Davion seemed to have it all figured out.

"Dave, I don't think you've thought this through. You should take some time and think it over. Just because you guys have a baby doesn't mean you have to get married." Ronald was trying his best to discourage Dave.

"I have thought about it dad, and I want to marry Tia so we can raise our son together," Davion said. At this point, I decided to speak up in support of our son.

"Ronald, most young men his age would run from this responsibility, but Dave is running toward it. Don't you think that's an honorable thing to do?" Ronald hesitantly agreed with me and gave Davion his blessing. Tia was a beautiful, sweet young lady. She reminded me of nineteen-year-old Jackie—soft-spoken and a bit shy. I was happy because I was finally getting the daughter I always dreamed of having. She even had a beautiful singing voice. But the most exciting part was that we had a grandson! Daylin was the happiest baby I'd ever seen. His nickname was Cheesy Boy because he was always smiling. I spent a lot of time with Tia and Daylin while Davion was either working at the bank or in the studio.

It had always been my experience that any time the phone rang between the hours of two and five a.m., it was undoubtedly bad news. When both my grandmother and my father died, it was in the early morning hours that I received the call. One morning around three o'clock, the phone rang, and it was Tia. When I saw her name on the caller ID, I couldn't breathe.

"Mom, don't worry—he's alright. But Davion was in an accident." Tia knew that it was best to reassure me before hitting me with the news. Even then, my heart fell into the pit of my stomach and I sat straight up in the bed.

"What happened?" I asked.

"He fell asleep at the wheel."

"Did he hit someone?" I was thinking of all the possible scenarios, trying not to think the worst.

"No, but he smashed into a bunch of parked cars," she said.

"Oh my God! A bunch of cars? How many exactly?" Tia explained that he had hit three or four cars, but only one was seriously damaged. Fortunately for him, Davion was driving a 1998 Buick Roadmaster, one of the biggest, sturdiest cars ever built. So even though the car was totaled, Davion walked away without a scratch. I had been in the habit of praying daily for God to protect my sons, and I knew that night that God had indeed answered my prayers.

~

In the early nineties, there was a mass exodus from California to Las Vegas, Nevada where many were finding better homes and a lower cost of living, and some friends of ours from church were among the migrants. They were able to purchase a home for a little more than we paid for ours, but it was three times as large. Ronald and I began to discuss the possibility of relocating our family as well. I had been working for the church for nearly fifteen years and felt like it was time for a change. We decided to drive to Las Vegas to scope out the land and Davion and Tia went with us. When Davion realized that they could afford their own place in Las Vegas, he decided that's where he wanted to be. Davion worked as a teller for US Bank, and they had plenty of openings, so transferring his job from Los Angeles to Las Vegas was a simple process. The cost of living was so much less there, and it was not a problem for them to afford their own apartment. The original plan was to find new jobs of our own, sell the house, and join our children in Las Vegas, but that never happened. Instead, we ended up spending twice as much that year on gas and putting a whole lot more miles on our car driving back and forth to see our son and his family.

We should have learned our lesson with our oldest son and his failed marriage. But because we were so immersed in religious culture, we simply chose to believe that getting married was the right thing for Davion to do, and that everything would work itself out. We soon learned just how naïve our perspective was. At 19 years of age, Davion was not ready to be a husband. He made the commitment because he had seen his parents work through the most difficult of circumstances and seemingly come out on top. He wanted to be there for his son in the same way that his father had been there for him. He understood clearly the importance of the role a father played in the life of his son, and that was his focus.

After a year in Las Vegas, it became clear that Ronald and I would not be making that move, so Davion and Tia decided to come back to Los Angeles and move in with us. It was painful for me to watch them struggle, hurt one another, fail, get back together and fail again. But I was in the process of one of the most difficult things I ever had to do, learning how to let go and allow them to navigate their own way. I found joy in the fact that I now had two daughters, and the two of them became like sisters. Between three brothers and four sons, most of my life was spent surrounded by an overload of testosterone and I was simply not a girly-girl. I spent much of my childhood following my brothers around. I had also spent much of the boy's childhood doing things like playing basketball or racquetball or play fighting with them.

Tia and Sir's wife Kelly were some of the softest, sweetest girls I'd ever known. The more time I spent with them, the more I enjoyed cultivating my girly side. At the age of 40, Tia taught me how to apply eye shadow for the first time in my life. I thoroughly enjoyed spending time with my daughters. Unfortunately, Davion and Tia's marriage ended after eight years of trying to fill a role for which neither of them was prepared.

One of the most difficult aspects of being a parent begins once your children are grown. When they are young, you enjoy a certain degree of control over what they may or may not encounter. You have some involvement in most of their decisions. But once they become adults, you have no choice but to allow them to find their way and navigate their path. Even when they are making a wrong turn, you are powerless to stop them. It's like being just out of reach as you watch your five-year-old fall off of his or her bike.

While Davion was finding his way as a husband and father, Daniel exercised his amazing gifts to deliver a stellar performance during his senior year at Inglewood High. He accomplished his goal of getting straight A's and earned the highest SAT score in the entire school. Daniel had always been extremely competitive. Whether it was sports, music, karate, or academics; he refused to be beaten. When it was time to send out college applications, he chose to apply to both USC and UCLA. USC offered him enough of a scholarship to cover half his tuition, while UCLA offered him a full ride. He made the obvious choice.

Daniel wanted to have the complete college experience, so he chose to live on campus during his freshman year. As a parent, the only thing that can prepare you for when your child leaves home is faith. I had to believe that we had given him all the tools he needed to handle life on his own and make wise choices. I also had to be confident that even in the times when he didn't choose wisely, he would still be okay.

Though music was his first love, Daniel chose to major in business. The music program at UCLA was heavily classical, and would not necessarily help him in his career, considering the style of music he preferred. He believed that being a business major would be beneficial when it came to that aspect of his career, but soon realized that the direction of the required courses was not resonating with him. The economics classes of the business major made him feel like he was studying to become an accountant. At the same time, he was thriving in his Spanish classes. Daniel decided to switch his major to Spanish literature. He thoroughly enjoyed studying a foreign language, however, music remained his priority.

With Daniel living on campus, I had to adjust to not seeing him every day. At first, it was more difficult than I'd anticipated. When your babies are kicking you from the inside, and you fall completely in love, it's hard to picture them becoming independent of you. When you are holding them in your arms, you can't imagine the day they move out of your house. When you are spoon-feeding your little ones, you're not thinking of the day they leave the nest, and you only see them occasionally. But that day had come, and I had to watch as my brilliant little baby boy drove off in his silver Honda Civic. I tried to act like it wasn't that big a deal, but inside I felt as if I was losing a piece of myself.

Whenever the phone rang, I hoped it was Daniel just so I could hear his voice. He didn't call as often as I would have liked, but he did check in at least once a week. He also came home on most weekends, usually to work in the studio. One day, in the middle of the week, Daniel came to the house to visit and sat down at the piano.

"Come here mom, I wanna play you this song I just wrote." I immediately dropped what I was doing and sat down to listen.

"I used to say never, would I love this way, never, give my heart away. Never would a player hang his jersey up and leave the game . . ." The level of excellence at which my son was writing blew me away. I shouldn't have been surprised; excellence was a part of his nature.

Daniel wrote the hook and his friend, Emmanuel, helped with the verses. Davion helped to complete the bridge. They recorded the demo immediately, and along with many other songs they had written, they were able to get a publishing deal with Warner Chapell music. As dedicated as Daniel was to his education, he was equally as dedicated to his music.

EMMANUEL "CHIZ" CHISOLM

Daniel met Emmanuel when he was five years old. His mother was a member of the church we attended, and they were in the same kindergarten class in the children's church. They didn't get along well because Emmanuel was always bragging about how his brothers knew the hip-hop group Bone Thugs-n-Harmony, and that he was a rapper. Although they saw each other every Sunday for several years, they didn't really connect until Daniel started attending a new middle school, Warren Lane. He didn't know anyone and felt relieved when he saw Emmanuel walking by himself. "Emmanuel?" Daniel called out his name, not sure if it was him. "What's up, Daniel?" He was relieved at the response. Emmanuel was still the same braggadocious kid with a chip on his shoulder, but it didn't matter. He was the only kid Daniel knew, and they stuck together. They both performed in the eighth-grade talent show. Emmanuel did a song with his then partner, Ozzie. The two of them made up the rap duo called Rated PG or RPG for short. They performed their single "Pushing 90," a song about speeding through LA streets and freeways. The irony was that this was three years before either of them would sit behind the wheel of a car. Daniel performed a classical piano piece and took first place. RPG came in second. They also took twins Tierra and Cierra to the eighth-grade prom together, dressed in their pin-striped suits with matching hats. Daniel wore burgundy and Chiz wore royal blue.

The two of them attended Inglewood High, and their friendship expanded into a partnership, forming a rap duo. Daniel made beats and Chiz would rap over them. They did everything together, from playing on the baseball team, dancing on the church youth dance team, academic decathlon, and eventually, student government. When they became seniors, Daniel was voted student body president, and Chiz earned the position of vice president. They were both true leaders in their class.

Daniel became the head of a group of young men called *Brothers or Nothing Else*, or B.O.N.E. But they weren't the only one of their kind. There was another clique that seemed threatened by their popularity as a crew, and the rivalry began. Chiz was most vocal about how much better they were in every aspect that mattered in high school. The friendly banter bubbled up until words and eventually turned into fists thrown. This resulted in one of their lead crewmates, Evan, being sent to continuation school, apart from the regular campus. It wasn't long before things calmed down and they eventually ended up graduating with honors. As president and vice president, they both spoke at their graduation, which was held at the Great Western Forum.

Chiz went to California State University, Northridge and Daniel attended UCLA. While in college, they'd leave their respective campuses and meet up to write music together. They received an ASCAP award for writing and producing *Never*, recorded by an artist named Jahiem.

~

Sir Darryl finished high school with a bang. But like his brother, Davion, he decided that college was not for him. He started working first for Bally's health club and then L.A. Fitness as a salesman. Within the first year, he was promoted to manager. Kelly was working in the accounting department at Big 5 Sporting Goods and attending school part-time. The two of them moved in together. This time, Ronald and I didn't say a word about marriage. We had learned our lesson. The days of making choices for our sons were over. We had only to make suggestions, give advice and pray that they chose wisely. But that wasn't always the case.

All of our sons were aware that drugs were the reason that their father spent seven years in prison. So, the thought never crossed my mind that they could even be tempted to try them. We believed that taking them to church every Sunday and keeping a close eye on them throughout the week would be enough to protect them from that element. They were all excellent students, and other than the episode with Davion, we never had any real disciplinary problems out of them. So, it came as a complete surprise when we found out that Sir Darryl had gotten caught up. He always had a mind of his own and was determined to do things his way. He couldn't just take our word for it, he had to find out for himself that drugs were the enemy.

He appeared to be doing well on his job. For a while, he worked at the West Los Angeles location of the health club on La Cienega near the 10 freeway. I purchased a membership, mainly to support him. And because there was a chiropractic office inside the gym, I had a good reason to stop by weekly and check on my baby. After several months, he was transferred to the Hollywood location. The drive from Inglewood to Hollywood was too far for me to continue my weekly visits, and before I knew it, months would go by without me seeing my son. He would fail to answer my calls for weeks. I remember picking up the phone and making another attempt to check on him and, when he didn't answer, I felt a heat that began in my chest and radiated up to my head and out to my limbs. In the same way that my mother knew when something was wrong with me, I knew that something wasn't right with my baby boy, and I had to go see about him.

me that she was no longer living with
about him. She gave me the address
ying.

LA Fitness anymore?" Kelly stated.
anything about his life right now."

now how he's doing when you get up there?"

I could tell by the sound of her voice that there was a lot more that she wasn't saying. At that moment, there was nothing more important to me than finding my son and making sure he was okay. I immediately got in my car and headed for Hollywood.

Although he was a very independent and self-sufficient young man, Sir Darryl was only nineteen years old, and he was still my baby boy. I could not bear the thought of something happening to him. The drive felt much longer than usual.

Traffic was extra heavy, and it seemed as if I was getting caught by every red light. It was a struggle to keep from being overcome by fear and anxiety, so I told myself to relax and trust that nineteen years of consistent prayer for my son had been enough. Still, I felt the need to have a conversation with God, and then with myself. I asked God to protect him. Then I inhaled, and whispered to myself, "relax Jackie."

I arrived at the address that Kelly had given me. It was unusually close to Hollywood Boulevard, which was not a good thing. Based on the shoddy condition of the building, I didn't know what to expect. I made my way up the stairs and knocked on the door.

"Who is it?" I recognized my baby's voice and was relieved that he was there, but I wasn't ready for what I saw when he opened the door. Sir Darryl was 5'11" and normally weighed about 200 pounds. But the person that answered the door was a frail, gaunt, 160 the strong young man that I had raised.

"Hi mom," he said with a forced, semi-smile. He tried h appear as if everything was okay, but we both knew it wasn't. I cou when he opened the door that there were at least five or six rand people lying around in what appeared to be a pile of trash.

"Come on in," Darryl said in an uneasy tone.

"No, thank you." I gave him a long hug and told him that I just came to check on him. I knew immediately that I had to get my son out of that place, but I wasn't sure if he would agree to come with me. I called Davion and told him to meet me there, then went around the corner to a Subway restaurant and waited for him to arrive. When he did, we went back to the apartment to rescue my child.

Sir Darryl had always had a mind of his own. Other than things like "do your homework," "clean your room" or "go to bed," there were not many times when I had to tell him what to do. Today, however, was different. I knocked on the door.

"It's me again Darryl."

"I'll be there in a minute," I could hear people shuffling around as if trying to fix the place up before opening the door.

It took a bit longer than it should have for him to answer the door this time, so I knocked again.

"Darryl, what's going on?" I was beginning to worry. A moment later, he came to the door.

"Hi mom," he said again, this time trying his best to look normal. I reached out and grabbed him again, embracing him tightly and whispering in his ear.

"You're coming home with me," I said, in a matter-of-fact tone.

"Okay. Let me just grab my clothes." He had no objections. In fact, I could tell he was relieved. He wasn't the type of young man to ask for help, but he certainly welcomed it when it arrived. He gathered his things that were haphazardly strewn all over the room and put them in a large plastic trash bag. Sir had been spiraling out of control for several months, and he welcomed the opportunity to move back home and regroup. I never asked him exactly what he had been doing. I knew from my own experience with drugs that he didn't need a lecture from me. He was already beating himself up for making such poor choices. I was confident that all he needed was a change of environment and to be surrounded by his loving family. Once his head was clear, Sir Darryl was quite capable of finding his way back to a straight path. Once he had eaten and showered, Sir went right to bed. He slept for the entire evening, woke up, ate dinner, and then went right back to sleep. I was at peace because my baby was safe at home with me. I was confident that everything was going to be all right.

It wasn't long before Sir was in the studio again just like his brothers. This time, he was committed to doing his own thing, creating his own sound and pouring his heart and soul into the passion of music that was undeniably rich in his DNA. He was able to restore his relationship with Kelly and after a few months at home, the two of them found an apartment not far from us in Hawthorne and moved in together. Over the next few years, their bond became stronger than ever.

It was during these years that each member of the Farris family was thriving in their own way. Sir Darryl kept busy with any odd job he could find at the time, while he continued to work on his music and develop his unique style. Kelly was still working in the accounting department for Big 5 sporting goods store and together, they laid a solid foundation for their lives. Ronald was enjoying his job at the L.A. Mission. Helping men to overcome their addiction was his passion, and he was very good at it.

All of the guys wrote and produced songs as a team as well as individually. They got placements with many different artists, including a song by the Pussycat Dolls called *Takin' Over the World*, from their *Doll Domination* album.

Daniel spent the summer of 2006 in a Spanish immersion program in Costa Rica. I knew that he was wise enough to take care of himself, and I tried my best not to worry about him. Our boys had grown into young men, almost completely independent of their parents. I felt good about the direction they were all headed in. It was evident that we had given them all we had, and it was now up to them to decide what to do with it. One of our proudest moments as parents came in 2007 when Daniel had finished all of his undergrad coursework and it was time for him to receive his bachelor's degree. Upon his acceptance to UCLA, he was invited to speak as an incoming freshman at the Black graduation ceremony. Now, as a graduating senior, he was asked to speak once again. This was an extremely special occasion because, up to that point, no one in our immediate family had graduated from college.

In the days leading up to the graduation, Daniel read his speech to me a few times to get my opinion. It was filled with passion and a spirit of activism motivated by the lack of Black faces on the UCLA campus. He would only read the first half, and then say the rest is a surprise. I couldn't wait to hear what he had come up with. On the morning of graduation day, before I could even get to the kitchen and make my cup of coffee, the tears of pride and joy began to flow. My baby boy had completed four years at UCLA, one of the most prestigious colleges in the country, and he was graduating with honors. He was fluent in Spanish and had become a leader among his peers. Daniel was setting a precedent for our family, which is still being followed by the younger members of the Gouché-Farris clan.

My mother lived alone in an apartment in Compton and told Daniel that morning that she was going to sit this one out because she wasn't comfortable driving all the way to Westwood.

"Bambama, you are not about to miss this! I'm coming to get you." Daniel drove to Compton to pick his grandmother up. The entire family gathered at the house on Park Circle and, after taking pictures and having our pre-graduation family celebration, we caravanned our way from Inglewood to Westwood, to the UCLA campus. The long walk from the parking lot to Royce Hall was somewhat difficult for my mom, but we were all so elated over the occasion that it didn't matter one bit. We just took our time, enjoyed the scenery, and breathed in the beauty of the day.

The Black graduation ceremony was quite unique in that it was as much a celebration of Black heritage and African culture as it was the achievements of the students. Instead of *Pomp & Circumstance*, the processional was led by the festive beating of congas and djembe drums, followed by dancers dressed in traditional African attire. Instead of blue and gold, the scarves around the necks of the students were Kente cloth. The room was overflowing with black and brown faces all filled with pride, but none prouder than the Farris family.

Daniel appeared early in the ceremony and we all cheered as they introduced him to speak on behalf of his class. He stepped up to the microphone, first acknowledging everyone that was there to support him, beginning with his father. Then with as much humor as eloquence, he described the experience of being Black at UCLA shared by many of his peers. Daniel spoke of the activism that had become a regular part of his life, and his passion for ensuring admission to universities like UCLA for students of color. Then, Daniel Farris became D Smoke!

"We gon' scream at the top of our lungs like we crazy, they try to shut us down so come on let's fight! We gon' bling like the diamonds we are, they so shady, we try to spread love and they block our light. But let it ring in the atmosphere that we Black and we just won't act like we happy here! Don't make me pull the mack out and blast in here cuz I will straight bring the hood to these Westwood hills . . . BUT WAIT . . . I'm an educator, so let's get real. We gon' march 'til we numb and we can't feel our heels. We gon' stroll likes Greeks and we roll like wheels. We're only several hundred deep, but still . . . you gon' feel me! Now admissions, listen. By excluding my people I admit you don't know what you're missing. Probly just a good ol' academic ass kickin' cuz my last math test, man I SET the curve. And I bet you just scurred to let us in, but stand corrected, Black pre-health is perfecting medicine. This school is like a raisin and now we 'bout to moisturize and add flavor cause they lack melanin. So let's act like we know what's hap'nin'. We gotta stand up cuz our rights got revoked! Let's uplift our people, and let'em know they just ticked off the wrong Negro, D SMOKE!!!

My first year, I thought I was a 'G', but this racist institution made a revolutionary outta me! Along with many others, my sisters and my brothers. So let's pump the fist together, LET'S GO! CLASS O' 07!!!!

In that moment, while the crowd was cheering and my family was hugging and high-fiving one another, the memories of Daniel's unique life flooded my mind. I thought about the day he was born and the dreadful, yet beautiful circumstances surrounding it. I thought about that little strong-willed toddler who refused to stay in the playpen, and the fights he got into as a young boy. I was tickled when I remembered him telling his grandmother *"I gotta talk!"* And as I watched the remainder of the ceremony, and my son and his classmates received the honor that they had all worked so hard for, once again, the tears of gratitude and pride began to flow.

Between his family and his peers, Daniel must have taken a few hundred pictures as we slowly made our way from Royce Hall back to the parking lot. Then we headed straight to our favorite restaurant, the Cheesecake Factory in Marina Del Rey. Our party was quite large, at least nineteen or twenty people, so we had to wait for them to set a place for us on the lower patio, around the fire pit. For the next few hours, the Gouché-Farris family celebrated Daniel's incredible milestone as we ate, talked, laughed, cried, and even sang! It was one of the most unforgettable occasions ever. Daniel shared with us some of the little-known details of his college journey. He told us not only about the times he aced the tests and scored the highest, but also about the time he mispronounced the word *epitome* in front of the whole class, and the shame and embarrassment he felt as a result.

~

Our first priority as parents had always been to provide our sons with the stable, loving, happy home that we both longed for as children.

Our relationship with one another took a back seat to ensuring the well-being of our sons. The more independent they became, however, the deficiencies in our marriage slowly began to surface. We soon realized that loving God, going to church, and living sober, moral lives was not enough. Neither of us had developed the skills required to nurture a healthy relationship. No one had taught us money management, or how to communicate effectively. We had not learned how to deal with the damage caused by our addiction and the resulting trauma that was still affecting us. Up to this point in our lives, all of our energy was focused on being good parents, and we were succeeding at that. But we were failing at marriage.

When Ronald first went to prison, leaving me as a single mother, a storm began brewing in my soul. I was angry because of the countless nights I spent soaking my pillow and I resented Ronald for not being there. But this anger and resentment had been neatly tucked away so that I could experience the joy of parenting. Still unaware of this storm, it hit a peak when Ronald left his job at the L.A. Mission and finances became extremely tight. For a while, mine was the only consistent income in the household and my stress levels were through the roof.

The property value had skyrocketed after we purchased our home on Park Circle and we took out a second mortgage. The loan officer was a minister friend of ours from church so we naïvely trusted that we were making a good move. This was our first experience with homeownership, so we were unaware of the dangers that lurked in the mortgage industry. The loan was an adjustable-rate mortgage, and when the rate changed, we could no longer afford the payments. This was the home in which Ronald was raised, and the only home that Ron Ron had ever known. It was located in the heart of Morningside Park, in Inglewood on the coveted Park Circle, and we were losing it. The strain that this put on our marriage was too much for me. Ronald and I initially moved out of the house and into an apartment on the West side of Inglewood. Our sons were now twenty, twenty-one and twenty-two, and capable of taking care of themselves.

The guys continued to grind away at their music, but things were not panning out the way they'd expected. They linked up with a few different managers, each of them confident that they could make the Farris brothers and the Woodworks team the "next big thing." They met and wrote with different producers and worked in some of the most lavish studios in Hollywood. They were able to land a few significant placements, none of which seemed to enhance their status in the music world. They ultimately reached the point where they decided to take their careers into their own hands.

After having had enough of being handled by industry managers and being disappointed by empty promises, they decided to work with Emmanuel's older brother, Shaun Chisolm. Rough around the edges, Shaun was anything but an industry guy. This made him the perfect candidate for the grassroots movement they sought to create. The first thing they needed was a place to set up shop; a central location to record, strategize and just chill as a team. They called it a "mound," referencing Jay Z's line *"we need a place to pitch, we need a mound."* Shaun Chisolm offered them exactly that.

Shaun didn't cut hair, but he was a hustler. He provided space for his peers to clean edge-ups, sculpt fades, and trim beards in the front while his younger homies chased their dream of building a musical empire out of the back room. It was no bigger than four hundred square feet, but it served as a creative space, as well as a place for them to lay their heads at night. As painful as it was, we all had no choice but to take the loss of our home in stride and keep it pushing. In the storage area in the back, Shaun kept a 5-unit t-shirt press where he would create merchandise for them to wear at shows and events, as well as offer product to their fans.

As fate would have it, just as their musical endeavors took on a new phase, Daniel received an $86,000 check for writing and producing the song, *Never.* Before the money arrived, they experienced bouts of frustration, applying for day jobs, selling newspaper subscriptions, and wondering about their chances of success. Daniel, however, took it as a sign that they should keep going forward. In a decisive act of leadership, he purchased a fifteen-passenger van, wrapped it with the faces and contact information of the Woodworks team, bought a concert-ready sound system and a couple of pieces of equipment to improve their sound quality. These investments reinvigorated them and gave them confidence in their new direction.

Daniel describes the spirit of Woodworks during that time, and the subsequent events:

"As we rode around in our new, we could feel the energy from the local community. They knew we were here. They knew we were up to something. That year we performed all over the Los Angeles area, from the Whisky-A Go Go Club in Hollywood to performing and panhandling at Venice Beach and the Santa Monica Promenade. We still knew we needed a great deal of exposure and we were willing to earn it one show at a time. There were plenty of times when we set up our sound system in open spaces and performed, using a generator and live instruments.

All while this was taking place, Shaun Chisolm's youngest brother, my childhood best friend, was rapidly diminishing from complications caused by rounds of chemotherapy and radiation treatment. After working together for a few years, a disagreement about a deal we were offered led us to pursue our musical careers separately. Interestingly enough, his brother continued to manage me and my crew while his second eldest brother Mark helped him to create Akadame Records as he worked toward putting out his debut solo project entitled "Rap School for Dummies."

After having been in a group with him for two years, I was well aware of his challenges with lymphoma, but we all just knew he would beat it. He was young and had a lively spirit. Little did I know that during the months while we focused on our separate endeavors, Chiz would suffer a rapid decline. Within a week I got some of the best and worst news I could have received. Kendrick Lamar, one of the top up-and-coming rappers on the West Coast, was performing at the Whiskey a Go Go and needed openers. Of course, we confirmed and would go on to rock one of our best shows to date. However, in that same week, Sean Chisolm walked into the studio. "When was the last time you went to see Man?" he asked. We called him Man, short for Emmanuel. I told him it had been some months, but we had talked recently. I was still in the habit of checking in to see how he was doing.

'You need to go see him while you still can.' I could see in his face that it was dire.

That week, the night before the show at Whisky a Go Go, Tiffany and I rode out to Chiz's house to visit him. When we got to the door, his fiancé, Brittney, greeted us with a warm hug and offered us some water before calling for Chiz. We sat on the couch and waited for him to come out, sensing morbid energy in the room. Chiz walked out slowly wearing a hospital gown that he had taken home. His skin was pale and he looked as if he weighed less than 100 pounds. Below his sleeves, sores peeled from his arms as his body fought to expel the rejected treatments.

Despite all of this, he smiled and greeted us as if all was well.

'Wassup yall.' He said.

'What up Chiz.' We both responded, fighting to keep our faces from showing the heartbreak that we were enduring. We made small talk about what had been happening at the studio and he told us of his complications, but he spoke as if he was still optimistic about the outcome. He informed us that he had decided to go completely natural since the medicines had prevented him from being able to digest food and left him feeling weak. He congratulated us on booking the show opening for Kendrick Lamar.

'That's the perfect crowd for y'all," he said. He went on to say, 'if I'm up and about I'm gonna pull up to the show.' At that moment, it took everything in me not to break down. The smile he maintained was the only thing that kept me from breaking. We didn't stay long, knowing that he was slightly uncomfortable being seen in that condition. Before we left, we told him we're praying for him and that we loved him. He reassured us of the same and we left.

The next day, we killed the show at Whisky a Go Go. We got love from the crowd, who yelled for our CDs as we threw them from the stage. We then broke down our equipment and got drunk, knowing that our friend was not well and of course, did not show up. Two days later, Emmanuel was admitted to the hospital. This did not come as a surprise. By this time, we knew what was inevitable. I visited him once just to let him know how proud I was to be his friend, *and then I went on teaching at View Park High School by day and writing songs by night.* Two days after I visited him in the hospital an administrator called me out of class where I was teaching at View Park High School. They informed me that they'd hired a sub and that a family member was there to see me. I walked out of my classroom and saw my uncle Funzell. He had never visited me at work before. At that moment, I knew what happened but still waited for him to confirm it. 'Chiz passed *away* last night shortly after midnight.' He hugged me as I cried on his shoulder."

After losing our home, my anger and resentment that had been neatly tucked away for so many years came rushing to the surface. After four months of living in that tiny apartment, it reached a boiling point. I could no longer stay with Ronald, so I filed for divorce and moved into my own apartment. We had overcome drug addiction and incarceration and successfully raised four responsible young men, but our relationship as husband and wife had come to an end.

As if losing our home wasn't devastating enough, the end of our marriage struck a painful blow to just about everyone who knew us, especially our sons. Although they were old enough to understand my decision, they didn't like it. Ron Ron was particularly hurt when I left his father. We had been together for two-thirds of his life, and he didn't know how to handle the fact that our relationship was over. It broke my heart to know that my decision caused so many people so much pain, but the weight I was carrying had become too heavy for me.

While my marriage to Ronald had come to an end, Darryl's relationship with Kelly had only grown stronger over the years after high school. She was a no-nonsense source of stability for him. She refused to stand by and watch as he engaged in self-destructive behavior, but she was right there to pick up where they left off when he was ready to settle down. It warmed my heart to see them together again. Kelly was good for Sir Darryl, and for that reason, I loved and appreciated her. In the Summer of 2009, Sir Darryl decided to make his relationship with Kelly permanent. He asked his father and I if we would help with the wedding. They didn't want a big ceremony, they just wanted to be married so we all decided to make it a family affair. The wedding was held at my apartment and Ronald officiated the ceremony. Kelly's sister helped her shop for a dress, bouquet, and veil. Tia did her hair and make-up. Even though Kelly was the bride, she still insisted on cooking a Jamaican feast with her sister Debbie's help. Despite our divorce, coming together to celebrate our children was never a problem.

~

Since the divorce so much about my life had changed. I loved God and my spiritual core was still intact. But with a failed marriage and the loss of our home, so much of the way I'd been taught to believe didn't seem real anymore. However, each Sunday I was still expected to lead the congregation in praise, no matter how I felt inside. On the surface, I seemed to have it all together. I had a successful career in music and a job doing what I loved to do. I had four beautiful sons, but deep down inside I was miserable. I wanted desperately to simply go to church, sit in the audience, and cry until the pain subsided. But each Sunday I put on my best smile and asked God to help me lead the congregation in genuine, sincere worship.

I was living in a one-bedroom apartment in an upscale complex called The Heights on Centinela and La Cienega on the West side of Los Angeles. My rent was fifteen hundred dollars a month, which was a stretch for me. When I told Daniel that the two-bedroom apartments would cost only six hundred dollars more than I was currently paying, he agreed to be my roommate. I was confident that all of my sons loved me, but Daniel was the most supportive. My relationship with each of my sons was unique. I related to Daniel as a friend as much as I did a parent. Although I had been able to handle things quite well when Ronald was away, there were many times that I found myself pouring my heart out to little Daniel. Even at the age of ten, he had the presence of mind, as well as the wisdom to not only lend a listening ear but also to offer me words of encouragement. Now, as director over the SHAPE program, he had become like a counselor to me.

My marriage wasn't the only thing I had given up on. I had given up on myself. I no longer felt qualified to lead worship, but music was the only thing I knew, and I couldn't afford to quit my job. I had lost all hope of having a career as an artist. I was forty-five years old and believed that my season had passed. There were a few things that still gave me a sense of self-worth. Confident in my intellectual gifts, I decided that I would go back to college and begin working towards a degree in psychology. I felt like music was too much of a hustle at my age, and I had to work very hard to put on a happy face to continue in my position as a worship leader.

The one thing that made me feel good about myself was the fact that I was the mother of some amazing young men. They were working very hard, and clearly on a path to success. I was confident in their ability but had given up on my own. Daniel, on the other hand, saw so much more in me than I was able to see in myself. I told him about my plans to go back to school and become a psychologist and he seemed slightly annoyed with me.

"Mom, you are trippin'! You're amazing! Your gift is still as prolific as it's always been. Do you have any idea the effect you have on the people at church? You are so anointed! And you're still beautiful!" His words were as much of a rebuke as they were encouragement.

"I'm going to produce a project on you!" he declared. My heart didn't want to agree, but because I trusted my son, I went along with his plans. Besides, it pretty much didn't matter what I said. Daniel's mind was made up and, just like the little eight-month-old in the playpen, I knew better than to argue with him. The thought of being a gospel artist at this stage in the game was extremely challenging. However, the fact that my son was going to be the producer made it all make sense.

Within a few weeks, Daniel had several tracks for me to listen to. He had solicited the help of both of his brothers, as well as his cousin, Tiffany. And when they began playing some of the tracks for me, I was pleasantly surprised.

"Wonderful Savior, matchless Creator, all-powerful you are. I was so tainted, felt so ashamed that, I thought I had gone too far. But You were there when I had let go, Your grace and mercy, they overflowed. Whenever my strength would fail you'd take over, I'm so happy I know ya. All praise to you I'm no longer bound, not saying my problems aren't still around. But when I feel the road I travel's too hard, I remember there's nobody like my God!"

Davion had written the first verse and the hook to this song. He sent it to me in an email and then asked if I liked it.

"Do I like it? Are you kidding?? I LOVE it!!!"

I was amazed at how my son was able to capture my sentiments in these lyrics and put them to a track that I never could have created on my own. Davion sang it as a demo for me, but his voice sounded so beautiful that I insisted we make it a duet.

Before I could process the pleasant surprise that I had just received, they sent another one. This time it was a song written by Daniel and produced by my niece, Tiffany Gouché called *Big God, Little Me*. They sent me the track, with the hook already done. I completed the song by writing the verses and the bridge, and Daniel even added a rap verse. This pattern continued for a few months until we had finished a project that I was extremely proud of, with *Big God, Little Me* as the title track.

"Sun, moon, all the hosts of heaven, earth, sky, they declare the glory of God, my God. He is sovereign and holy and unto the only wise God be majesty and power. He who sits upon His heavenly throne . . . alone, brought salvation to all who believe. Every valley shall be exalted and every mountain and every hill made low. The crooked made straight and the rough places plain, all in the power of His name. BIG GOD, little me! The Creator of everything that you see. Beyond eternity, still perfecting everything concerning me. BIG GOD, little me! The only one who is able to set you free. One God in the Trinity. SO BIG, but He inhabits the praises of little me!"

The re-launch of my musical career was off to a pretty good start. I was traveling around to different churches, playing, singing, and leading worship, teaching in seminars, and selling product. People were constantly being blessed as I shared the gift that God had given me, but I was still floundering in my personal life. My newfound single-ness afforded me a freedom that I had never encountered as an adult, and there was nothing in my previous experiences that could have prepared me for it. I was like a kid in a candy store, and though the idea of dating had been somewhat foreign to me, it was time for me to learn what it was all about.

I began exploring all of my options. This included signing up on dating websites and going to the club on Fridays, as well as meeting men at random locations like grocery stores and the gym. Because of my religious background, and the fact that I got married at the tender age of 21, I felt like I'd missed out on a vital part of life, and it was time for me to catch up. Meeting men was effortless. Having someone take me to dinner or buy me drinks was fun. But after several months of dating, drinking, dancing, and catching up, it started to feel empty. I thought I was ready to find someone to settle down, but finding someone attractive enough to pique my interest and wise enough to keep it, well, that was a lot easier said than done.

While I was enjoying my singleness and dating a series of different men, Ronald hated the idea of being single and living alone. At the beginning of 2009, he set out to find someone to replace me. Vanessa was conveniently located at the church he was attending, and they began dating. The following summer, Ronald was appointed as a pastor over a small church in Altadena. As a spiritual leader, he had to be careful to follow all of the rules, including the prohibition of pre-marital sex. So, he proposed to Vanessa, and she accepted. He was looking for a salve to ease the pain of divorce and the loss of our home, and he believed a wife was what he needed. It wasn't long before Ronald learned that his marriage to Vanessa not only came short of meeting his needs, but it also came with a whole list of complications for which he was completely unprepared.

Although Ronald has never been the type of man that would cheat on his wife, Vanessa was extremely jealous. No one could convince her that he wasn't having multiple affairs. At one point, he went to perform his duty as a pastor and comfort a family who had just lost a nineteen-year-old girl, killed by a drunk driver. He was at the home of the grieving mother trying to minister to her, but his cell phone kept ringing. Of course, it was Vanessa. He ignored the first four calls, but on the fifth one, he decided to step away and answer his phone. He excused himself and stepped out the back door into the laundry room. Vanessa could hear the noise of the washing machine when he answered her call.

"Baby, I told you I was going to visit a family. Now, what's so important that you keep calling?" He tried to keep his tone from sounding too annoyed, knowing that would only make matters worse.

"What's that noise?" Vanessa paid no attention to his question. She stood ready to accuse him of infidelity.

"What noise?" Now he truly was annoyed.

"You're bangin' somebody right now, aren't you?!" Ronald couldn't believe what he was hearing. She mistook the sound of the washing machine as the sound of him having sex with another woman. He knew at that moment that he had rushed into what now appeared to be a hopeless situation. Over the next few months, the accusations continued and with the end of that year also came the end of his marriage to Vanessa.

Ronald began having an occasional drink, which at first seemed harmless. Then, in 2011 he was involved in an auto accident and had to have surgery on his back. The pain he experienced gave him a reason to drink even more. From 2010 to 2012, Ronald's drinking slowly escalated from a few shots now and then, to a daily ritual. At least three or four days each week, he hung out at the Karaoke bar, often drinking to the point of blackout. He would experience periods ranging from a few moments to several hours where he couldn't remember anything he'd done. Despite rebukes from his sons and his sisters, this unfortunate pattern continued until September 29, 2012, when everything changed.

On the way home from the Falcon Bar in Manhattan Beach, at around three in the morning, Ronald stopped to get some cigarettes. That fateful moment at the gas station at the intersection of Jefferson and Crenshaw is where Ronald opened himself back up to his old friend, addiction. He had been drug-free for more than twenty-three years, but once he put that pipe in his mouth, he fell back into his compulsive behavior as if to pick up right where he left off. After a few weeks of getting high, his sisters convinced him to seek help, so he checked himself into the Veteran's Administration hospital where he stayed for twenty-one days. Afterward, he was sent to a live-in treatment center called the Bimini House.

Since we were very young, both Ronald and I believed firmly in God and His Word. We have also come to understand that knowing and walking with God does not exempt you from life's challenges, difficulties, and failures. It does, however, give you a guidance system to navigate your way through them, and help you come out stronger, wiser, and better in many ways. In hindsight, it is evident that this guidance system was at work even when Ronald was drinking and getting high. During his stay at the VA hospital, Ronald learned about VRAP, the Veteran's Retraining Assistance Program. It provided him with a monthly education allowance of fourteen hundred dollars.

Many of the men at the Bimini were former gang members and ex-cons with a much more colorful past than Ron's. There were also several veterans who were taking advantage of VRAP and going back to school. Ronald was inspired by the fact that they seemed to be thriving in the program. Some of them were even straight-A students. Once he got settled into the Bimini, he made a real commitment to his sobriety and his education.

After having more than twenty-three years of sobriety under his belt, it was humbling for Ronald to start counting again from day one. He came across men in the program that he had counseled when he was working at the L.A. Mission. They knew him as Chaplain Farris but now he was one of them, just trying to get his life back on track. When they found out he was a pastor, they even requested that he begin teaching bible study in the program, but he declined.

"I'm not here for that, I'm here to focus on my recovery," he explained. Ron was well aware of the work that it was going to take for him to successfully overcome his addiction, and he wasn't going to allow anyone to distract him.

Between 2010 and 2012, Ronald and I didn't communicate much at all. He was busy working on his relationship with Vanessa. When his marriage ended, he knew exactly what he wanted, and he decided to come after it. At this stage in the game, I was not even considering the possibility of getting back together with him. But Ronald knew me well enough to know exactly how to get my attention.

I was finishing up the *"Big God Little Me"* project with Daniel when Ronald called to see if there was anything he could do to help. In addition to his educational stipend, he was also receiving insurance money from his auto accident. As if that wasn't enough, he had money coming in from financial aid, all while living rent-free at the Bimini.

"Hey Jackie, I know you're working on music with Daniel. I can help you with some of the expenses." I was surprised at his offer. It seemed to come out of the blue, but he was being strategic. He had been with me through all of the ups and downs in my career and he knew how much it would mean to me for him to contribute to my success. I immediately accepted his offer, and he began paying for one thing after another. By the time the project was complete, he'd spent more than five thousand dollars, which was a big deal at the time.

Besides helping with my music, Ronald offered to take me out to dinner, often. "No strings attached," was his favorite promise. I'd made it clear that I wasn't interested in anything other than friendship, and he was willing to be my friend. After dating several different men, none of whom were husband material; spending time with him was refreshing. I knew exactly who he was, and even more importantly, I knew he loved me unconditionally. We would go to dinner, and the movies off and on for several months, but while Ronald was working on rekindling our old flame, our sons were busy grinding away at their music.

RONALD FARRIS I   **DANIEL "D SMOKE"**

CHAPTER SEVEN
MUSIC INDUSTRY

Once Daniel received his first big royalty check and invested it in the van and sound equipment, it was time to make another move. After spending several months living and working out of the tiny space provided by Shaun, it was evident that the space was no longer sufficient, so Daniel took advantage of an opportunity to rent a storefront space on Manchester and La Brea in Inglewood. It was about nine hundred square feet with a tiny bathroom in the back and a loft upstairs. It was being used as a storage space for construction material. The floors were half-finished, recycled tile riddled with cracks and smeared caulk. Random planks of wood and metal sheets leaned up against the wall over a half-empty can of paint. Sitting in the back near the wall were two brown leather chairs with yellow padding bursting out from the holes in the fabric. The walls were painted several different colors as if the previous tenant couldn't decide which direction to go in and used all of them. There was no art, no cohesive vision, no purpose, yet Daniel still saw unlimited possibility.

Daniel and Sir spent the next several months making countless trips to Home Depot for supplies. They completely gutted the place, stripping it of all the old furniture, paint cans, wood planks, tile, and metal sheets. Then step-by-step, Daniel and Sir built the unit into the place of business they'd envisioned. They installed laminate wood floors panel by panel, then erected a brick façade on one of the main walls to create a rustic effect. They installed mirrors on the wall opposite the bricks, framing them with wood paneling that they measured, cut, sanded, stained, and finished themselves. Once the room was nearly complete, they commissioned a local artist by the name of Ms. Huggy to do a mural of Aretha Franklin, Miles Davis, John Coltrane, and Ella Fitzgerald. They erected a 12-foot scaffold so she could reach the height of the wall in the section with the vaulted ceiling. As she outlined her masterpiece, they played their music for her and described the vision for the space.

It took them four months, but they completely transformed the place into a functioning multi-purpose storefront with a recording studio. The main room was rented out for dance classes, rehearsals, or video shoots. He also allowed other brands to sell their clothing, hats, and jewelry there, taking a cut from all the sales.

The most exciting thing that took place at Woodworks happened every Thursday night, the same night I held choir rehearsal. It was an artist's movement called Bass & Treble. Each week the event was hosted by one of the members of the Woodworks team and featured another. Either Tiffany would host, and D Smoke would perform, or Davion would host, and Sir would perform. They would also have an additional guest artist each week. Some of the most brilliant talent in the industry showed up for Bass & Treble, including Robert Glasper, Terrace Martin, Kenyon Dixon, Alex Isley, Iman Europe, Iman Omari, Sha'Leah Nikole, and a host of others.

Woodworks had quickly become a hub for the industry in the city of Inglewood. And though everyone on the team was enjoying its success, it was still Daniel's studio. Davion wanted to do something independent of his brothers so he decided it was time to branch out on his own. He rented a spot nearly an hour away, in Van Nuys, opening a studio called the *Red Room*. Word had gotten around about the Farris brothers and the Woodworks camp, so when news spread of Davion's spot in the valley, he began to attract a whole new set of industry people. Like Woodworks; Davion would hold mixers, parties, and events where artists could come and showcase their talent. Luke James, Steve Russel, and Eric Bellinger are just a few of the artists that graced the Red Room.

My brother Andrew was working as music director for Chaka Kahn during this time and he hired me as one of her background singers. We did a three-week tour in Japan, visiting Tokyo, Osaka, and Sapporo. I was unable to continue traveling because of my job at the church, so Davion took my place. His first background vocal gig was for Oprah's 2011 karaoke contest winner, Abraham McDonald. That tour took them to the Netherlands, Switzerland, and Tanzania. He also toured Israel, Iraq, and Kuwait singing behind Chaka Kahn. When he wasn't on the road, Davion was writing, producing, and doing shows at the Red Room or Woodworks studio with his brothers and his cousin Tiffany.

Davion had been the first of his brothers to master the art of studio engineering, and when he wasn't working as a songwriter, producer, or background vocalist, he was earning a living as a studio engineer. He coached both Daniel and Sir in the process of learning how to navigate the recording programs, but Sir Darryl wanted to take it a step further. He believed in being the best at whatever he did, so he decided to enroll in the Los Angeles Film School. Within two years, he graduated with an Associate degree in music production.

In the process of learning how to engineer, he was also developing his style of music. Although Sir had been the one of all my boys who protested the most against music lessons, he was still absorbing everything I taught him, and it began to show as he started writing and producing his own songs. He would create a track, and then ask his brother's honest opinions. It wasn't always good, but it caused him to quickly grow into an amazing songwriter.

"I keep having the same old dream, it's the one where you're with me." He used his parent's divorce as inspiration to write the song from the perspective of his father, as a man who continually dreamt that he and his wife were still together.

"You were wearing that red dress . . . that I bought you for Christmas. Baby just seeing you kept on reminding me of everything that I loved. I was holding your hand and . . . we were somewhere romantic. I went in for a kiss—but as soon as I did girl you disappeared—damn!"

Sir played that song for me and I nearly lost my mind. It was truly one of the most brilliant songs I'd ever heard, so I knew right away that his gift was real and prolific. All I could think about were the dozens of times that I had to either beg, bribe or threaten him to get him to sing with his brothers. I didn't really expect him to pursue music as his passion, but it became clear to me that the problem was never a lack of love for music, he just didn't like being told what to do. From the time that Sir Darryl was a toddler, he wanted to do things his way. From using the potty on his terms to the toys he chose to play with, Sir always had a mind of his own. And if his brothers were doing it, he wanted to do something else.

It gave me great joy to see Sir Darryl in the studio, and even greater joy when I heard what he was able to do. Not only did he write brilliant lyrics, but he was also an amazing singer and a masterful vocal arranger. I was now certain that, despite all of his protests and rebuttals, he had been paying attention when I was giving them vocal lessons, training their little ears, and teaching them music theory. It was almost as if there was an internal compass that was guiding him back to his musical destiny.

Sir Darryl applied for odd jobs to support himself and his wife while in pursuit of his musical goals. He got a job selling rugs, but that didn't last very long. He also tried his hand at selling newspaper subscriptions, but thoroughly hated it. He finally got a job as a salesman for the Guitar Center in the South Bay area near Los Angeles. It was the perfect position for him because of the discount he received on his equipment. Sir would work on his job during the day and his music at night. In 2015 he released a project called *Seven Sundays* on a label called Fresh Selects, which immediately created a buzz in the industry. He would perform at different venues throughout Los Angeles, and although the project was somewhat successful, he kept his job at the Guitar Center.

TDE

Dave Free, a manager at Top Dawg Entertainment (TDE) an established independent record label, happened to be with someone who was playing Seven Sundays. He was impressed by Sir's music, so he reached out to Kenny, the owner of Fresh Selects, and asked him to set up a meeting. Kenny immediately called Sir Darryl.

"Hey man, you know where Santa Monica is?" Kenny asked.

"I'm in Culver City right now," Sir replied.

"Well, Dave Free and Kendrick Lamar want to meet you. Can you pull up right now?"

"I'll be there in fifteen minutes." Sir immediately headed to Santa Monica for his first meeting with TDE.

When he arrived at the meeting, everyone was chill. Jay Rock, Dave Free, and Kendrick Lamar were all there. In the first few moments of small talk, Jay Rock informed Sir that they were related.

"Man, we're cousins!" Jay Rock declared.

"How so?" Sir was intrigued.

"Your Auntie Linda is my Auntie Linda!" It was as if Jay Rock couldn't wait to make the connection. He continued,

"Her husband, Uncle King is my uncle, my blood uncle!"

"Wassup Cousin!" Sir replied. They both laughed and shook hands as if they'd known each other for years.

The meeting went exceptionally well. Sir played more of his music and Dave Free was even more impressed with him at the end of the day. They began discussions on the possibility of signing Sir to their label, and within four months, the deal was secured.

~

Daniel's job as director over the SHAPE program at UCLA came to an end and he was offered a position at Inglewood High School as the

Spanish teacher. Ms. Tate was still the school principal, and she was excited to have her former student fill the position. African-American men that can teach Spanish are hard to come by in Los Angeles. Daniel had not yet obtained his teaching credential, but there was a stipulation that he could take the job as long as he was enrolled in a program. When Daniel told me that he would be teaching at Inglewood, I was excited and proud. After congratulating him and telling him how proud I was, I immediately offered some motherly advice.

"You know you're going to have to be careful, right?"

"What do you mean?" He replied.

"Never allow yourself to be in a compromising position with those young girls," I explained.

"Trust me mom, I already know," he confidently assured me.

I knew that Daniel was a respectful, wise, and responsible young man, with a character that would not allow him to intentionally get caught up in some mess, but it wasn't him that I was concerned about. It was no secret that some of Daniel's students would find him attractive, and some might even actively pursue him. I just didn't want to find myself in a position to have to strangle some young girl for lying on my son.

"Just make sure you're never alone with a female student!"

"Okay mom," he agreed. Daniel never had any issues with the girls in his class, so my worries were unfounded.

Daniel taught at Inglewood High School for two years, then one year at Westchester High School. He took a break from teaching for a while to work on his music, but when he was offered a position at View Park Preparatory High School, he decided to go back to teaching. After teaching there for a year, Daniel accepted an offer to teach at Augustus

Hawkins High School located on the South side of Los Angeles at Sixty-Fourth and Hoover. This proved to be a challenging job for him because the culture was different from any school he'd ever worked at.

"Mom, please pray for me." he said and I could tell by the sound of his voice that he was serious.

"Why? What happened?" I said as I took a deep breath to try and slow my heart rate.

"How am I supposed to keep from punching one of those disrespectful-ass students in the face?"

"You know you can't do that Daniel!"

"I know mom. I would never actually do it. But I wasn't quite ready for what I have to deal with in the classroom," he said as he went on to express his frustrations.

"I have some really great kids in my class. But I also have some knuckleheads. I spend so much time dealing with the difficult ones that it's unfair to the ones who are serious about learning." I listened as he outlined his issues, wishing I had the answer, but I didn't. Without having ever been in his position, I had no idea what to tell him. But what I did know was that he was going to figure it out. He always did.

Although he enjoyed teaching, music was still Daniel's first love and he was committed to his career as an artist, songwriter, and producer. Each day when the clock struck three, he immediately switched modes from Mr. Farris to D Smoke. Even with the success of the studio, building their catalog and fan base was hard work.

~

THE SECOND TIME AROUND

Up until I was nine years old, my life was perfect. I had two perfect parents, two very cool brothers, and a German Shepherd named Buddy. We all lived in a beautiful home in the city of Inglewood, California. But that perfect life ended when my parents got a divorce. For the next ten years, the one thing that I longed for more than anything in the world was for my parents to get back together. The dream of being a family again didn't end until my father died. But my longing for the wholeness of the family was something that I still carried with me, even beyond my own divorce.

Six years had passed, and Ronald had not only gotten his life back on track, but he was also thriving. He worked full-time as a counselor at the Bimini House where he originally lived as a client and he attended school full-time as well. Our friendship had blossomed into something we'd never experienced, and we were spending more and more time together. It was as if our sons were the center of gravity that continued to draw us together.

In July of 2015, he was planning a trip to Jamaica to celebrate his sixtieth birthday, and he invited me to go with him. I reminded him that we were still only friends and that if I agreed to go, we would be sleeping separately.

"I don't have a problem with that. I know we're friends, and I can't think of anyone else I'd rather spend my birthday with. I promise to keep my hands to myself," he vowed. I took him at his word and agreed to go on the trip. It was an all-inclusive resort, and we had a suite with a private pool and an ocean view. We swam in the pool, relaxed in the jacuzzi, went on a boat ride and snorkeling excursion, rode horses at the beach and I even swam with the dolphins. We sang in the Karaoke bar and dined at each of the five-star restaurants. We had an amazing time together and just as he'd promised, he was a perfect gentleman.

On the day before the last day in Jamaica, Ronald wanted to go ziplining and I just wanted to lay on the beach. He knew I needed some alone time, so he did not try to pressure me into going. The entire time we were there, Ronald didn't mention the word marriage, but it was an unspoken issue. We had spent twenty-five turbulent, wonderful, miraculous, challenging, beautiful years together. And the six years we'd spent apart were equally as challenging. It was during that time that I learned that the lovely green grass on the other side of the fence was actually artificial turf and that my own yard could be healthy and beautiful only if I nurtured it.

In my two-piece bathing suit and tropical sarong, I laid out on the cushioned chaise lounge in the private cabana and listened to the sounds of the ocean. With each wave, I was overwhelmed with the thought that I wanted my husband back. I wasn't even sure exactly where that thought was coming from. Possibly because of the innate desire to be a family again, as a result of my parent's divorce. Or maybe because I believed that no one would ever love me like Ronald did. Despite his faults, failures, and struggles, Ronald was a good man with a kind heart. He was an amazing father, and I was certain that he would lay down his life for me. So, immediately upon our return home, we began devising a plan. There would be no fanfare, no public announcement, and no church wedding. We simply wanted to reconnect what had been severed.

The following week, Ronald and I went down to the county clerk building on Imperial Highway in Inglewood to apply for a marriage license. Once that step was complete, we called our friends Dwight and

Kathy and arranged to have the ceremony at their home, with the only guests being our sons and their wives. Ron Ron, Shavonne, Darryl, Kelly, Davion, and Daniel all stood around as Dwight led us in the process of fixing what we had broken. In addition to our relationship being restored, we were also able to purchase another home within three months. Life was good.

~

Every Thursday night after my choir rehearsal, I would head to Woodworks studio, which was located less than a mile from the church. In awe of just how much they'd grown musically, I enjoyed watching my sons do their thing. The crowds always spilled outside the door and even down the street. Bass & Treble had become a major event in the city of Inglewood and my babies were at the center of it. Woodworks studio was the place where magic happened each week. It was also the place where Daniel, Darryl, and Kelly would lay their heads each night.

For the first ten years after graduating from high school, Davion, Daniel, and Sir Darryl were grinding away at their goal of a successful career in music, often sacrificing the stability of a job with a regular paycheck and benefits to pursue their dream. They forfeited basic luxuries, like a kitchen and hot shower in their home. They spent countless hours in the studio creating and developing their unique sound. They performed wherever they were invited, most times without pay so that they could build a following and solidify their brand. When they did work jobs that had nothing to do with music, it is certain that the majority of their pay was turned into investment money to fund their dreams.

The boys were signed to DreamWorks Records in 1995. Now, twenty years later, Sir Darryl was once again signed to a label, this time as a solo artist. His first release, "Seven Sundays," gained a decent amount of traction and succeeded in getting the attention of Top Dawg Entertainment. He then released "Her & Her Too" in 2016. Each record contained some notable songs, such as "Queen," "Ooh Nah Nah," and "Westside Boi." Since he was a little guy, Sir was always the most laid back of his brothers, and having a record deal didn't change that. All the while he was doing shows, shooting videos, and promoting his brand, he held on to his job at the Guitar Center until he was established as an artist and was certain that music would take care of him and his family.

It was Sir's 2017 release of *November* that began to bring him to the forefront of the music world.

Tell me who dat nigga if it ain't me? If it ain't a party then it's finna be. Never had a problem that I couldn't solve. It must be official if I get involved. Quarter pound of fire burnin' daily. Harder to remember, getting harder to remember. I been through enough to drive me crazy. I don't think my mama's gonna save me. Maybe I'm not flyin' but I'm floatin.' If we're not headed to the top, where we goin'? Two miles an hour can you picture me rolling. Cause life is so much better when you live in slow motion. One spliff a day-a keep d'evil away-a, ca one spliff a day-a keep d'evil away-a.

Sampled in dozens of songs by several different artists, this familiar Caribbean chant by a young artist named Billy Boyo got the attention of Sir's listeners on a song entitled *D'Evil*. The video for this song was shot in Jamaica and attracted more than 12 million views. Immediately after its release, TDE took its artists on the 2017 *Championship Tour.*

This tour featured all of TDE's artists including Kendrick Lamar, SZA, Schoolboy Q, Jay Rock, Ab-Soul Lance, Skiiiwalker, and SIR. It was called the "Championship" tour because of the sports theme. Each artist represented an all-star from different sports, with Sir as the baseball player. Top, the "T" in TDE, went all out with this tour, including shooting commercials to advertise it. It began in Vancouver on the fourth of May and ended in Burgettstown, Pennsylvania on the sixteenth of June in 2017. The most exciting day of the tour for me and my family was May 15th, when they performed in the City of Inglewood at the Great Western Forum.

For fifteen years I had been driving by the Forum and taking a different route to avoid the traffic on the days when a major artist was scheduled to perform there. I'd taught my sons to drive in the parking lot and attended a Prince concert there. Home of the Los Angeles Lakers basketball team from 1967 to 1999, the Forum was an iconic venue with seating for more than seventeen thousand. Its stage had been shared with the likes of the Jackson 5, Stevie Wonder, Barbra Streisand, Bob Dylan, Kiss, Paul McCartney, the Bee Gees, Parliament Funkadelic, Alice Cooper, Fleetwood Mac, Jimi Hendrix, Led Zeppelin, Elvis Presley, and a host of others. My excitement was indescribable when I drove by the Forum on my way to church and saw several giant banners like sports jerseys hanging on the outer wall, each with the artists' name at the top and a number in the middle. Sir's was number 7.

The day before the concert, Davion and I took a special trip down to the Forum just to take a good look at the forty-foot advertisement with Sir's name on it. We were both so proud, we took selfies and videos in front of it. The day of the concert was even more exciting. Sir made special arrangements for his parents and siblings. Daniel, Ron Ron, his wife Shavonne, Davion, Ronald, and I met in the parking lot near the will-call booth to pick up our tickets and back-stage passes. And even though Kendrick Lamar and SZA were the main headliners, Sir's performance was flawless. As soon as the crowd heard the familiar Caribbean chant, *One spliff-a-day a keep de evil away-a,* they all began to sing along. The feeling was surreal!

But this was only the beginning. The next year, Sir would release another project entitled *Chasing Summer,* in which he featured Kendrick Lamar, who was now at the top of the rap game.

"Baby I'm just tryin' to let my hair down. Baby I'm just tryin' to let my hair down. Everybody's watchin' I'm aware now. I can't find a reason I should care now. Baby I'm just tryin' to let my . . . if I take off my cool, would you promise to stay? If I give you my heart, would you throw it away? Do you mean what you say when you tell me you love me? Do you really? Do you really?"

Hair Down became a major hit, selling more than five hundred thousand records and receiving over thirty-three million views on YouTube. I knew Sir Darryl was brilliant. I knew he made good music. But I had no idea the degree to which he had grown into his gift. Ever since he was a toddler and insisted on going in a different direction than his brothers, I wanted little Sir to be as passionate about music as I was. He always complied when I asked him to sing, but he never really seemed to be enjoying it. It wasn't until after he graduated from high school that I began to see his true musical potential.

The most laid back of his brothers, Sir never came to me and said "Mom—guess what?" One day I just looked up, and there his face was on a massive billboard in Times Square. I would be walking in a store, or sitting in a restaurant, and I'd hear my son's voice on the radio. People would be singing along or dancing slightly. It seemed that my baby boy was more popular than I realized. I found the greatest joy in watching Sir fall head over heels in love with music and carve out his unique lane.

THE NOVO

In November of 2019, Sir Darryl called and told me that he wanted me to sing in one of his concerts.

"You want me to sing background?" I asked.

"No. I want you to sing a solo." I immediately felt nervous.

"What do you want me to sing?"

"That's up to you. You can sing whatever you want. It could be gospel—something you wrote maybe. I don't care, it's up to you."

I spent over twenty years singing behind different artists. I'd traveled all around the world and stood on stages in front of thousands. I was also accustomed to leading worship on Sundays and singing solos each week. But performing in front of a crowd of young hip-hop fans was not something I'd ever imagined myself doing, especially at my age. But I was presented with a challenge, and I was prepared to face it head-on.

"I want you to sit at the keyboard and do what you do!" Darryl said with a smile. His confidence in me was enough to boost my own. Now I just had to figure out the perfect song. I wanted to be true to myself, but at the same time, sing something familiar to the audience. I knew it wasn't a "gospel" crowd, and most of them would not be familiar with my music, so I chose one of my old favorites.

"You can reach me by railway. You can reach me by trail way. You can reach me on an airplane, you can reach me with your mind. You can reach me by caravan. Cross the desert like an Arab man. I don't care how you get here just, get here if you can."

This song had become a part of my life when Ronald was locked up. When it first came out, not only did I fall in love with Oleta Adams' voice, but I also connected with the lyrics because I wanted my husband to come home. So, this was a performance that I would be able to pull off with all my heart and soul.

The day of the concert I was a nervous wreck! I wanted to make my son proud and, of course, not embarrass myself in front of the two thousand plus people that had come to see him. He had also invited some of the artists featured on his record to perform that night as well as his brothers, Davion and Daniel, so I felt the pressure to be great. I spent several hours trying to find just the right outfit, and even more hours at the piano practicing exactly what notes to sing and play, so I could look and sound my best.

On the way to the venue, I was completely overwhelmed with fear. I didn't even understand the level of nervousness I was experiencing, so I began a conversation with myself.

"Jackie, you GOT THIS! You've been doing this for over thirty-five years. You are a Pro. You know what to do. Just go out there, sit at the keyboard, and do YOU! You're going to be great!"

There was a four-hour space between sound-check and perfor-mance, in which I repeated those words to myself at least a thousand times until the fear went away. When it was time for me to sing, Sir commanded the audience's undivided attention and said simply, *"Watch this!"*

He sat on the floor of the stage beside my keyboard as I played and sang, looking up at me like he had done when he was a little guy. I could see the love in his eyes as I confidently executed what I had been preparing for my entire life. And when it was over, the response let me know that I had done exactly what I set out to do, make my son proud.

~

While Sir Darryl's career was taking off, Daniel's was taxiing on the runway. With more than 20 years of experience in the music world, he understood that he could not accomplish his goals and reach his desired destination alone. He had already developed relationships with some brilliant young minds that he'd met while attending college, so he began putting together his team. Greg was a sophomore when Daniel arrived at UCLA and assisted him in moving into the dorms for his freshman summer program. After graduating from UCLA, Greg helped local inner-city students get into many of the best colleges in the country before he attended Howard University School of Law, Greg and "Smoke" developed a friendship that eventually blossomed into a business partnership.

Daniel met DJ Shanxx at one of his Bass & Treble events. Shanxx became a regular and they would speak often. It became clear to them that they would eventually work together. Daniel respected Shanxx ability to navigate the business, and Greg's expertise in legal matters.

Daniel had been toying with the idea of incorporating Spanish into his music. Now fluent in Spanish, he decided that teaching would not be the only benefit of being bilingual. He tried out his Spanish rapping skills in front of an audience for the first time at the Whiskey a Go Go when he opened for Kendrick Lamar.

> *Si tu me entiendes te lo digo. Andar en mi zona eso es no mas suicidio Palabras afiladas como el vidrio Soy el caliente y tu eres no más tibia, Birria!*

The crowd went wild! At that moment it became clear to Daniel that he was on to something special, and he decided to run with it. He began writing a series of Spanish verses to sharpen his skill set. Daniel and his team came up with a plan to further promote his brand. Each week, for seventeen weeks in a row, he released a brief music video where he used his linguistic skills to rap in both English and Spanish, with the translation at the bottom of the screen. He called the series *Run the Subtitles*. This video series got the attention of the likes of Jill Scott, Tyrese, and DJ Battlecat, all of whom would repost them, sharing them with a much larger audience. Word of this talented young bilingual rapper began to spread until it reached the producers of a new show. I received a call from Daniel with exciting news.

RHYTHM & FLOW

"Hey mom, I got presented with an opportunity to be on a rap competition show. I'm thinking about doing it, I just don't like competitions. But it's Netflix . . . what do you think?" My first thought was to tell him not to do it. I don't like competitions either. But when he said it was Netflix, I started thinking that it could be a good thing . . . a very good thing.

"Netflix? Tell me more!"

"The judges are Chance the Rapper, Cardi B and T.I." The more he told me, the better it sounded.

"Wow!" I already thought very highly of the judges. I can't call myself a fan of very many current Hip Hop or R&B artists, but I have been a T.I. fan since 2012 when he released his *Paper Trail* CD. I would escape the pain of my divorce with *Live Your Life, Whatever You Like* and *My Life, Your Entertainment* playing in my headphones while I jogged around the bowl at Kenneth Hahn Park. My respect level rose even higher when I began to see his face in movies and television. I knew T.I. to be someone who made wise moves in the entertainment industry, and knowing he was a part of this show gave me a sense of confidence in what it might offer Daniel. Although I wasn't a fan of Cardi B's music, I did have respect for her journey. I also admired Chance the Rapper's independent rise to stardom. So, my advice to Daniel was, "I think you should go for it."

He expressed his concerns that it was "Reality TV" and had the potential to paint him in a different light. But when he was told that they could only use what he gave them, he agreed to participate. He made the conscious decision to limit his on-camera time to his performances and interviews. This would keep him from providing them with cheap fodder for tabloids. In the final edits of the show, his face is not even seen until just before it was time for his performance. His strategy included distancing himself from trivial interactions.

After auditioning for the producers and being officially accepted as a contestant, Daniel was thrilled to find out that, in addition to Cardi, Chance, and T.I., Snoop Dogg was going to be a guest judge at the LA auditions. The taping was held at a club in West Hollywood, and he invited his father and me to attend. Ronald was unable to make it because he had to work, but there was nothing to keep me from being there. I received an email with the address, parking pass, and arrival time. They told us to be there at 1:00 p.m. and that the taping was scheduled to begin at 3:00 p.m. Being punctual is a part of my nature, so I made it to the parking structure by 12:45 p.m. It was a few blocks away and they provided a shuttle to the venue.

It took a little more than an hour for them to open the doors, so it was around 2:30 p.m. by the time I was able to get inside and find a seat. Most of the audience stood around the stage, but I chose to sit in the back until it was time for Daniel to perform. The judges arrived an hour later, and the competition finally began.

The first contestant was introduced, and they came running onto the stage, interacting with the crowd the entire time.

"Get yo mutha-f-in' hands in the air." My first thought was, "oh God . . . here we go." Then one by one, the performers would run up on the stage and try to get the crowd hyped.

"Ay yo yo yo, make some mutha-f-in' noise!"

"WHAT THE F**K IS UP L.A. ? WHAT THE F**K IS UP? AAAAAHHHHHH!!!"

I probably heard that word more times during the show than I had in the past six months. But that wasn't the difficult part. When the show finally aired, most of the contestants had been edited out. We only got to see the faces of about twelve of the thirty that auditioned.

And only a handful of them made it through to the next round. It saddened me to watch as the judges crushed one dream after another. But it was necessary. Most of them had impossible dreams and someone needed to set them back on the path to reality. I've always said that if my kids weren't naturally talented, I would not have encouraged their pursuit of music. I would have suggested strongly that they become engineers or attorneys or something, but it was clear that their talent was undeniable in the first five years of their lives.

As much as I wanted to leave the club and take a break until it was Daniel's turn, there was no way for me to know whether or not he was next until his name was called. There were thirty contestants, and Daniel was number twenty-eight. So, I had to sit through the entire show and watch every performance. It was quite refreshing to me when DJ Head finally said the words;

"All right L.A., next to the stage . . . D Smoke!" Unlike all of the other contestants, Daniel walked on stage and calmly greeted the audience and the judges.

"What's up, what's up? How y'all doin'?" He didn't run. He didn't yell. He didn't try to hype up the crowd before his performance, he let his talent get them hyped. He was there to present himself as professionally as possible. Despite the instructions from the producers, he refused to allow anyone to make him do anything that did not come naturally to him. He's never been one to follow crowds or bow to peer pressure, nor did he have a problem disagreeing with authority figures, so he did what he felt was best.

I had been sitting off to the side near the rear of the building where I could barely see past the audience to the stage. More importantly, I had a clear view of the side of the stage where each performer waited to go on. As soon as I saw Daniel approach the stage, I made my way to the front. I stood only a few feet from the judges to the right of Snoop, watching their reaction the entire time.

"Listen, if your throat clear and your lungs open and it's Smoke that you need, one, two. He got hopes, fears, and he young focused, if he pull the thang boy gon' shoot! Went from broke years with the trunk open sellin' tapes like what we gon' do! But in four years he graduated with his B.A., now whatever he say translate."

It was funny to me when I watched the show several months later after it aired and realized that they edited away much of what actually happened that day. They also cut at least half of the audience's cheers after Daniel's performance, as well as most of the judges' reactions.

"So, D Smoke" T.I. said as he looked down at the card that described Daniel. "what do you do for a living?"

"I'm a teacher" he responded.

"What do you teach?" He wanted to know more.

"I teach Spanish and music production in high school." Then Chance The Rapper took over.

"It makes sense to me that you are a teacher. I could feel the mentoring vibe coming across in your performance."

They were all amazed by his talent and his energy and wanted to know more.

"It says here that you play classical piano?" T.I. said while looking down at the card in his hand.

"That's right" Daniel responded again. He continued.

"I thought it was incredibly different for you to incorporate Spanish in your art. As an executive, that shows me another stream of revenue, you know what I'm sayin?" The crowd responded with cheers and laughter.

It was now Cardi's turn.

"You know you really impressed me. Cuz when I first saw you, you looked like you was gon' mop some floors." Everyone seemed to be amused by her comment. But she went on to compliment him, especially his use of Spanish, and even suggested that he could write for her. The most intriguing moment of the night happened when it was Snoop's turn to speak. I was standing about six feet away from him and I could feel the energy as he spoke. He leaned back in his chair, crossed his ankle over his knee, and confronted Daniel.

"D Smoke, where you from homie?" His tone was serious.

"I'm from Inglewood," Daniel responded with certainty and confidence.

"Nah, where you from homie?" He asked again, this time with an almost threatening vibe. The audience wasn't sure what was going on, but Daniel understood exactly what Snoop was doing. It was a familiar challenge that Daniel and his brothers faced often while growing up in Inglewood. He knew that it was very real, so he responded with the very same words.

"I'm from Inglewood." After saying it a second time, except for a few chuckles, everyone in the room froze as if there were no cameras, no judges, and no audience, just two warriors in an intense stand-off. After a beat, Snoop lifted his sunglasses and looked Daniel in the eye, smirking as if to give his approval. Daniel smiled in return with his head still held high. The crowd then exhaled with laughter just before Snoop began to explain his gesture and acknowledge Daniels's brilliance.

"You know I had to ask you, you know. Just 'cause I wanted to see if you broke the chains. Niggas sweatin' you and checkin' you and asking you where you from . . . trying to draw you back into that negative world, and I see you wouldn't allow me to do that."

"Period," Daniel responded, with self-assurance and strength. After a few more compliments from Snoop, the baton was passed back to T.I., and his words were no surprise to me or anyone else in the room.

"Yeah man, this is an easy road. I wanna see you in the next level of the competition."

Daniel exited the stage as the audience continued to cheer him on. I made my way to the back so I could see my son before heading home. All of the contestants had only been allowed out of the green room when it was their turn to perform and immediately rushed back in, so neither of them was able to watch their competitors. I couldn't wait to tell Daniel just how brightly he'd shined. Our conversation was brief as the stage manager rushed him back to the green room to prepare for Old Man Saxon's performance.

"Baby!!! You killed it!!" I said as I reached out to give him a huge hug. Did I do alright?" he asked with a smirk.

"And Daniel, after what I just saw, you got this! I think you may actually win the whole thing!"

"Right now I'm just focused on getting past the next level."

In the second phase of the show, the contestants were put in groups of five, and each group performed as a team. They called it the Cypher. Once again, Daniel stood out amongst his peers and breezed on to the battle rap phase of the competition. At the end of each show, Daniel called me to tell me how things went.

"I made it through Mom," he said as if relieved.

"I knew you would baby." Even though I was unable to attend all of the tapings, I never doubted for a moment that Dan would make it through each round. After moving past the Cypher round, Daniel was set to battle Old Man Saxon. He wasn't looking forward to it because, despite the camaraderie that they had begun to develop, he knew that one of them would be going home that night. This was more of a problem than either of them realized because at the end of their battle the judges were in a complete quandary. When they stepped away to deliberate, they were gone for more than twenty minutes trying to figure out a way to keep them both on the show. They even called the attorneys to see if they could get around the established rules, but to no avail.

"The judges decided to go with . . . . D SMOKE!" This was the first time in the process where there was ever a doubt that he would move to the next level. He couldn't wait to call me and tell me the good news.

"Mom, I made it through!" I could feel the sense of relief in his voice.

"I feel kinda bad for Ol' Man Saxon. I'm just glad it didn't go the other way! And I'm even more excited about the next round. We get to shoot our own music video, and they've given us a pretty decent budget to do it!"

"So, you have to write a new song and shoot a video in one week?"

"Yup! But I can handle it. I already have the vision for it, and I'm working with an amazing director. It's gonna be EPIC!"

The joy of watching Daniel's progress in the competition kept me from being consumed by the problems in my relationship with Ronald. We had been reunited without consideration for the depth of our original issues, and I began struggling as soon as the excitement of having a new home started to wane. Ronald was unaware of many of my struggles because they were mostly internal and unspoken. The anger and resentment that had been neatly tucked away in the early years of our marriage didn't just disappear when we divorced. In fact, they settled in even deeper.

For three years I tried to pretend that everything was okay, silently suppressing my raging emotions and tiptoeing around Ronald to protect his feelings. I began to feel like I was choking and couldn't do it for one more day. So, I packed my things and moved out. I didn't necessarily want a divorce, I just needed space. But Ronald wasn't having it. He immediately filed for divorce and put the house up for sale.

"There's something in the water, something wrong. Something don't feel right, something going on, but we strong."

In the filming of his video, Daniel stands on the roof of our home while it was on the market. I was no longer living in the house with Ronald, and he was grappling with being blindsided by my decision to move out. Daniel's success was the silver lining in the dark cloud of our second divorce. The song he wrote was brilliant and the video was amazing. The judges loved it!

~

When Daniel called to tell me about the next round of the competition his excitement was contagious.

"Mom! Now we have to write a song using a famous sample. I'm going to use *Atomic Dog*, but I'm going to flip it and cut it in half!" Daniel seemed especially excited about this challenge, but I didn't hear from him again until after the taping of the show. He had been busy working on his song and preparing for his next performance. As soon as it was over, he called to tell me how it went.

"Mom . . ." I could tell by his tone that something was wrong.

"I went blank!! I forgot the lyrics!" My first thought was that it was over, and he didn't make it to the next round. I was about to give him the "You're still a winner" speech, then he continued.

"But they *still* loved me! They said it was the best song of the night, even though I messed up and forgot the lyrics. And when I say I messed up, I mean I MESSED UP! I forgot the whole second verse, but I made a nice recovery." I could feel his pain. As a performer, the worst feeling in the world is when you blow it in front of an audience. It's a combination of embarrassment, anxiety, and stress all at the same time. But I had never done it on that level, so I could only imagine what he must have been going through. I'm certain that the relief I felt when he told me what happened was nothing compared to his own.

While Daniel was preparing for the next round of competition, I was busy getting settled into my new apartment and working on my studies. I was in the final year of my Master of Divinity program at Azusa Pacific University, which was a blessing in so many ways. Not only did it give me something productive to focus on, but it also allowed me to accomplish my life-long goal of completing my education. When I first enrolled in the program, I had no idea just how much my life would change as a result. In addition to studying the Bible, there was a lot of coursework based on sources that either complimented or contradicted the Bible. This allowed us to gain a broader understanding of different world views, but that was only the beginning.

One of the required courses in the last semester was Pastoral Counseling. My first impression, based on the title, was that I was going to learn how to counsel other people. But that is not at all what this class was about. The purpose of this class was to take each student through a rigorous course of introspection and self-examination. We were guided through the process of finding our own broken places and initiating healing, to ensure that we were spiritually and emotionally healthy enough to counsel someone else. It was like a semester of group therapy, and it was intense.

I was forced to stand before a mirror and take a good look at all of me. I comforted the little girl who had been molested, confronted the teenager who had become promiscuous as a result. I congratulated the young lady who had won the fight with addiction and faced the pain of the young woman who was left alone for seven years to raise three baby boys. During this course, I realized that I had spent most of my life in a state of suppressed inner turmoil. One day when I went to the house to pick up a few more of my things, I got into an argument with Ronald. Something he said really rubbed me the wrong way, and for the first time in all of my fifty-five years, I spoke my truth without concern for someone else's feelings. I said everything that was on my mind, holding back nothing. It was as if all the pain he'd ever caused me came up from the place it had been buried, through my veins, to my lungs, and out of my mouth.

I felt like I was having an out-of-body experience as I stood over him, sobbing and screaming at the top of my lungs. In a fit of rage, I picked up the tray that was in front of him and slammed it down, knocking over the books and papers that were on it, all the while cursing and verbally chastising him for leaving me to be a single mother. I was aware that over fifteen years had passed since he got out of prison, but the hurt felt fresh. Fortunately for me, Ronald just sat there quietly and let me get it all out of my system. Neither of us expected the explosion that took place that day. And, after it was over, neither of us knew what to say or do. So, I just walked out the front door and went back to my apartment.

As soon as I drove off, I broke down again. Tears that I'd held back for fifteen years began to pour out and I cried from the time I got on the 105 Freeway at Vermont, until I pulled into my parking garage on Paramount Boulevard about twenty minutes later. Allowing myself the freedom to express my feelings fully was extremely cathartic, and a weight had been lifted. That night, I slept like a baby.

Ronald and I didn't speak to one another again until we received a call from Daniel.

"Hey Mom, I need all of you guys at the house tomorrow. They want to record some footage of the family together." He went on to give us specific details.

"They want to see us around the piano, and maybe looking at some family photos. Would you call everybody and tell them to be there at 3:00?" Daniel always relied on me to pull things together.

"Of course! We'll see you tomorrow," I replied. Though we were in the midst of some trying times, coming together as a family for something so exciting made it feel as if all was right with the world. The next day, Ronald and I were able to put our differences aside and just enjoy the moment. We went into the garage and pulled out the crate that held some of our most precious memories. Even though we were following the producer's instructions, it felt natural. Sitting around the piano and singing together was a regular thing and looking at old photos of my three little guys reminded me of just how far we'd come. Even though the house was up for sale, and the furniture we sat on was only staged, for an hour or so, it still felt like home. The tension between us always seemed to melt away when we were with our sons. Watching them thrive gave us both the greatest joy of our lives.

～

A few days later it was time for the final stage of the competition, and we were all invited. Ronald, Ron Ron, Davion, Sir Darryl and I arrived at the venue and were escorted to a designated waiting area for the final four competitors and their families. Daniel introduced us to London B, Troyman, Flawless Real Talk, and their loved ones. We all greeted one another warmly, and no one spoke of the underlying tension in the air. However, we were all well aware of the fact that the night would end in disappointment for three of the four rappers.

They were each allotted forty-five minutes for run-through and sound check. The producers asked the family members to be in the studio during this time for camera blocking, so we got a chance to preview Daniel's performance.

I knew better than anyone about Daniel's brilliant talent. For more than thirty years, I had a front-row seat to his diligence and commitment to excellence. I watched as he practiced piano for hours, while also getting perfect grades. I knew my son well and expected something great. But even I was blown away at what he did on that stage. As soon as I saw him sit down at the piano, I pictured my seven-year-old playing *The Spinning Song* in front of the church congregation and remembered the pride I possessed as his mother and piano teacher. What I felt at the current moment far exceeded pride. Daniel's skill as a pianist was evident as his fingers gracefully moved up and down the keyboard. With each note, I felt as if I were playing along with him. And the lyrics he had written hit as hard as they did because they came from a place of experience, a place of truth.

"This one's for love, for mothers that's grieving." With the loss of his childhood friend, Emmanuel, and a few of his high school classmates, Daniel was familiar with the plight of grieving mothers. *"It's for that dreamer in that class that's underachieving."* There were many times when Mr. Farris, the teacher, had to accept the fact that some of his students would never reach their potential. *"It's for believers whose faith is all that's keepin' 'em breathin'. It's the Garden of Eden, it's for all of my heathens.* Having been raised in the church, Daniel encountered many believers who'd seemingly come to the end of their rope but were able to hold on by a thread of faith.

This one's for Inglewood, both in Chicago and Cali. This one's for Manchester and Crenshaw, for Rally's. Happy moments happen to be sprinkled throughout half of these tragedies. Actually I just start embracing change. It's safe to say that growth is an uncomfortable process and pain is a necessary investment for progress. I stress that if ever you get ill, or hurt against your will, it's just a quiz from God, this is our test, ah yes. This time it's gonna be different. I'll bless the world with honest quotes in every sentence and get better every moment just like Beverly mentioned. Hard times but never resentment, I stay forever relentless.
LET'S GO!

Then, the beat dropped! Electricity filled the room, and everyone felt the shock! I glanced over at Davion, Ron Ron, and Darryl and saw the sheer delight in their faces. The tension between Ronald and I was non-existent. Together, we had created and cultivated an amazing work of art in D Smoke, and we both felt the love responsible for that creation.

"Keep it one-hunnid I be feelin' like Who? Who? NOBODY!"

Daniel Anthony Farris has always been in a class by himself. From the stubborn little toddler who refused to stay in the playpen, to the classical pianist in elementary school, to getting perfect grades in high school, to graduating from UCLA with honors, his entire life was miraculous. From the day he was born to a cocaine-addicted mother, only hours after she'd gotten high, to this one, it was clear that the hand of God was upon this young man. It was and still is upon the entire Gouché-Farris family.

Betty Jackson and Bartee Mitchell Smith were both blessed with the gift of music and it was intensified in their daughter and my mother, Betty Gouché. We didn't ask for it, nor did we do anything to deserve it, but that same gift continued to flow through me, my brothers, and all of our children.

Not only did God grace us with this incredible gift, but He also protected Ronald while he was incarcerated and brought him safely home to his family. It was God's hand that empowered him to become the incredible father that he is. It was God who kept Ron Ron from being caught up in gang life or ending up dead or in prison. It was only God who gave me the grace and wisdom to raise my young sons during my years as a single mother. He provided me with the resources I needed to take care of my family and continually opened doors for me in the industry. He blessed me to work with some of the greatest names in the music world.

It was God who gave both Davion and Sir Darryl the uncanny ability to sing, write, produce, and engineer. From Ron Ron to Sir, all of our sons are blessed with exceptional intellect.

For more than thirty-five years, Ronald and I fought our way through some of the worst of circumstances, often failing and making a mess of things. But we succeeded at raising four extraordinary young men. Despite our weaknesses, we gave our children all the love we had within us. We made them our number one priority, placing their needs over our desires.

In the introduction, I mentioned the law of cause and effect and the law of compensation. Love, discipline, and teaching are the seeds sown from the day that my sons were born that are now yielding the wonderful fruit of success. Loving your children means being attentive, patient, firm, fearless, putting your children's needs before your own, teaching your babies everything you know, and guiding them to someone who can teach them what you don't know.

The first time I saw each little face and felt the rapid heartbeat under their smooth, newborn skin, my heart began to beat more intensely than it ever had. For the first time in my life, I understood love. As the doctor placed those tiny people on my lap, the hairs on my arms rose as high as my temperature and the next breath seemed as if it were the very first time I ever breathed. The awesome responsibility of creating life gave me a true sense of purpose. I somehow understood that it was up to me to be the chief designer and architect of those beautiful little lives. When I look at my sons today, I am thankful to God that he allowed me the privilege of Raising Kings!

"SIR" DARRYL

ACKNOWLEDGMENTS

I am eternally grateful to God for allowing me to be born into a musical family. For orchestrating my journey and being with me every step of the way. For placing His gracious hand on my womb and shielding my children from . . . well, from me!

I am grateful to Ronald Farris, my children's father and forever friend. Our sons would not be the great men they are without having had you as their father. You were there the moment they took their first breath, and you've been there ever since. And I really, REALLY appreciate your financial contribution to the audiobook. I couldn't have done it without you!

I am grateful to my mother, Betty Gouche, for her love, support, and guidance. For always making room for my babies and me and for holding me together when I was unable to do it for myself.

I am grateful to you Ron Ron, for accepting me in your life as your "bonus Mom" and loving me with all your heart!

I am grateful to all those who contributed to this work. To Willa Robinson, thank you for loving this project almost as much as I do and helping me bring it to life!

To Sam Glaser, for the countless hours you spent recording and editing, and editing, and editing the audiobook! It was a labor of love! And thank you, Sam, for sharing your perspective. Your input was invaluable!

Last but certainly not least, to my Kings, Davion, Daniel, and Sir Darryl Farris. Thank you for just being awesome young men! For always striving for greatness and exceeding my expectations! Thank you for sharing your memories to help me tell OUR story. Thank you for being my inspiration, my reason, my glory, my joy, and my crown!

ABOUT THE AUTHOR

Jackie Gouche is a mother, mentor, minister, musician, singer, songwriter, and author. She has traveled to six of the seven continents while signing behind some of the most notable names in the music industry. These names include Elton John, Michael Jackson, Tina Turner, Diana Ross, Chaka Kahn, Quincy Jones, Patti LaBelle, Jill Scott, Yolanda Adams, and a host of others.

Jackie has also authored three books, including *How Would I Know*, her autobiography. *True Worshippers*, an in-depth treatise on the biblical aspect of Praise and Worship. In her most recent book, *Raising Kings*, Jackie candidly shares her experience as the mother of Daniel (D Smoke) Farris, Sir Darryl Farris (Inglewood Sir), and Davion Farris. These three young, Grammy-nominated artists are taking the music industry by storm.